Prai— f

Lov

"This book will encourage you to know that whatever the problem is, our past does not destroy our future and we can actually enjoy a friendship with God."

—Nancy Alcorn, founder and president of Mercy Ministries

"LOVED is full of precious stories that demonstrate God's ever-flowing grace, mercy and love. This book reminds us that He is always poised with open arms waiting for us to return to His embrace so He can heal our wounds and wash us in His deep, enduring love. These testimonies prove that love never quits, never ends and truly never fails."

—Leigh Devore, *Charisma*

"This collection of compelling stories is like a beautiful bouquet presented to readers with a life-changing message attached: *you are loved.*"

—Camerin Courtney, senior editor, *Today's Christian Woman*

"God is in every detail of our lives—the big and the small, the good and the bad. These amazing and inspiring stories will remind you of just how big our God really is and how He longs to carry you, heal you, and rescue you with that love. It is never too late!"

—Tammy Trent, recording artist, speaker, and author of *Learning to Breathe Again*

also by Rebecca St. James

Sister Freaks

Pure

Wait for Me

SHE

SHE Teen

NEW YORK   BOSTON   NASHVILLE

Loved

Stories of Forgiveness

Rebecca St. James,
general editor

WITH CONTRIBUTIONS FROM
Mary DeMuth
Elizabeth Jusino
Tracey Lawrence
Jennifer Schuchmann
Lori Smith

WITH A FOREWORD BY
Rebecca St. James

Copyright © 2009 by Alive Communications, Inc.

FaithWords
Hachette Book Group
237 Park Avenue
New York, NY 10017

Visit our website at www.faithwords.com.

Book design by Fearn Cutler de Vicq
Printed in the United States of America

First Edition: September 2009
10 9 8 7 6 5 4 3 2 1

FaithWords is a division of Hachette Book Group, Inc.
The FaithWords name and logo are trademarks of Hachette Book Group, Inc.

Library of Congress Cataloging-in-Publication Data

St. James, Rebecca.
    Loved : stories of forgiveness / Rebecca St. James. — 1st ed.
       p. cm.
    Summary: "A collection of true stories and captivating testaments to God's amazing
love."—Provided by the publisher.
    ISBN 978-0-446-19701-4
    1. Young women—Prayers and devotions.   2. God (Christianity)—Love—
Meditations.   3. Forgiveness of sin—Meditations.   I. Title.
    BV4860.S72 2009
    242'.643—dc22

                                                            2009003640

We were younger then, you and me, full of dreams, weren't we?

I went my way, you went yours, where did you go, dear?

Someone said you had left the life we lived together then

This is my way of reaching out 'cause I remember...

This is what I want to say to you

If I had one chance to speak to your heart

You are loved

More than you could ever know

This is what I want to say to you

If I had one chance to tell you something

You are loved

More than you can imagine

Imagine

If I told you would you believe, the narrow road, I did not leave

If I told you would you understand that I've found truth

Are you jaded? Are you hurting now? How I wish that I could tell

Where your heart's at... can you see? Mine has found—home

Not sure if I've, made it clear enough

It's not my love I sing about

Everybody asks, "Is God good?"

I believe, He is

In fact I know, He is

"You Are Loved" by Rebecca St. James

Contents

Part Three: Family Problems

Part Four: Friends

Part Five: Man Trouble

Part Six: Faith Crises

Foreword

When I was a child in Sydney, I had a friend named Daniel. I fell out of contact with him after leaving our Christian school to move to a different state. Years later, a mutual friend told me Daniel had fallen away from God and was going through a difficult and rebellious period. I was shocked and sad for him. When I was writing songs for the album that became *If I Had One Chance to Tell You Something*, Daniel randomly came to mind again—and I felt that this "random" thought was actually placed there by God. I had the concept: "If I had one chance to tell Daniel something, what would I say to him?" The message I felt God really laid on my heart was to tell him, "You are loved."

A few years have passed, and I think I understand the message even better now, explained to me by another friend, my life coach, Ken.

During one of our regular conversations, Ken gathered a wastepaper basket and a water bottle and brought them to where I sat on the comfy couch next to the crocheted pillow. He held the full water bottle over the empty basket-turned-bucket and began to slowly pour water into it. He asked me to try to grasp the water in my fist. I tried and wound up with only wet hands. No substantial amount of water remained in my hands at all. He then began to pour again and asked me to cup my hands under the water flow. This time my cupped hands began to fill with water and eventually to overflow. I was moved as a dawning realization encompassed my heart. My hands were in a position of receiving rather than grasping, being rather than doing; they were open palms rather than clenched fists. And this brought fullness, to the point of brimming over.

This is the way it is with God's love. For many years my walk with God centered around my performance. If I was doing what I thought I needed to do spiritually, then God and I were "good." And if I wasn't, then He was disappointed in me. I was grasping at God's love for me, rather than receiving it. I was trying to earn His love rather than graciously taking it and living for Him out of gratefulness for His goodness.

Our culture typically functions in this way: A + B = C. If I do this and that, then this desired end result will be mine. But God cannot be manipulated in this way. Spiritually, A plus B does not always equal C. Sure, we reap what we sow, both for good and evil. But just because we live to please God does not mean things will always turn out the way we want them to.

God's ways are higher than our ways, and the end result we hope for is not always what is best for us or what our loving Father will give us. The relationship with our "ideal" match may not turn out. We may not receive the job opportunity we think would be so perfect. But we need to see life from God's all-knowing, all-encompassing view. What we can count on, what He does promise us, is His love. A love that must be received, not earned. A love that involves surrender, not "getting it right." The women profiled in this book are wonderful examples of that love, receiving from God even when the "formula" indicates they don't deserve it.

Loved is a book about prodigals and for prodigals—which is all of us. God has His arms open wide, waiting for us, no matter what we have done. He wants us to run toward Him, and

He will run toward us. This is a message of hope that our generation needs to hear. No matter where you've been and what you've done . . . you are loved.

I've come to realize that, yes, we need to stand in awe of God and be blown away by His power. But His kindness and His love are really what draw us into a relationship with Him. His love makes us desire to know Him and to love Him in return. That is the most important message I need to share—through this book and in my life. From how I relate to others personally to what I say onstage, the message is, "We are extravagantly loved by God."

As the writers/creators of this book, it is our prayer that you, through this journey with us, will encounter God's extravagant love for you (see Romans 8:38–39). Ask Him to help you cup your hands and surrender, becoming open to the filling of His love. You are wanted and desired, created to bring joy to your Creator. He delights in you! Delight in His love.

Thanks to all who made the writing of this book a labor of love, and thanks to you, the reader, for coming on this journey with us.

In HIS love,

Rebecca St. James
Zephaniah 3:17

Introduction:

Before You Begin

This is a book about prodigals renewed—young women who have experienced firsthand the story of the prodigal son that Jesus tells in Luke 15. For a number of reasons and in a number of ways, these individuals fell away from their faith for a season, and then rediscovered the love of Christ.

Every story in this book is true, and the women are real, although we changed all names and certain identifying details to protect their family and friends. You will see some similarities among their experiences. Many of them suffered from the same temptations and walked the same dangerous roads. We have organized the stories to bring out some of these similarities and to examine together the crises and issues that can lead a woman down dangerous paths.

Each section is separated into daily readings and begins with a story called "In the beginning," which looks at a biblical woman who was affected by the same problems as those found in the modern-day stories that follow. Since the Bible doesn't always give us a lot of detail about the women, we've had to get creative with our retellings and imagine some of the details of those stories—such as facial expressions or the particulars of a conversation. But as much as possible, we've stuck to what the Bible tells us about these early prodigal women and the amazing ways God redeemed their sins and their lives.

Loved

part one

Identity Crises

In the beginning...

Rahab

*W*atching the foreign men who came and left her house, no one doubted that Rahab was "bad." Yet today this bad girl is so respected for her faith that her name is listed in the Bible's honor roll of believers.

Radical change is possible when God's love takes over.

Rahab was a prostitute. That's not a mistake or a mistranslation. The Bible actually says three times that she was a prostitute (or a harlot). Some have tried to downplay that ugly description, saying it really meant she was an innkeeper. But in her culture, "innkeeper" and "harlot" were often considered the same thing.

In a community where women were protected by their families, Rahab left the safety and security of hers to live alone. We don't know if she left willingly or if she had no choice. Maybe her parents disagreed with her moral choices and kicked her out, or perhaps she left voluntarily, seeking a freer lifestyle than the one offered in her society. Whatever her reason, she lived alone in a house built into the city wall—a prime viewing location for the local gossips. Everyone could see the men—both the locals and the travelers—who came and went from her house.

The foreign men who stayed with her must have told her about the world outside the walls of Jericho—a world where people didn't gossip about her in the streets.

She heard stories of the Israelites traveling in the desert, the miraculous parting of the Red Sea, and the recent overthrow of nearby cities. These strangers did not have temples as Jericho did and did not worship the many gods Rahab had always been taught to revere.

Is it possible there is only one God? An Almighty God? We can imagine that Rahab hungered for more information. And then one day someone knocked on her door.

"Come in!" She probably began clearing the flax off the bed to prepare for another customer.

Two men entered her home.

She sized them up and said, "Okay, but it will cost you double."

"Shhh. We're not here for that," said the one called Salmon.

They told her they were Israelites on a mission from God. She invited them in, though she must have realized they were spies. The Israelite army had been wiping out pagan cities along their path. Surely Jericho would be next, and these two men were here to scout out the best way to defeat her neighbors.

Yet Rahab let them stay. Maybe she was tired of the rumors and disapproval of those around her. Maybe she felt the heart-tug of the Israelites' God.

She probably gave the two men food and prepared a place for them to spend the night. But their careful preparations were interrupted by a pounding on her door. Messengers from the king—Rahab's king, the idol-worshipping leader of Jericho— were there to arrest Rahab's houseguests. Even the king started to look for foreign men at the house of the village harlot.

"Where are they?" the messengers asked Rahab. "Give them to us, because they are here to destroy us all."

At that point, Rahab should have turned the spies over. Anything else was considered treason, and treason was punishable by death.

But Rahab had never been concerned by the law, and she wasn't ready to sacrifice her houseguests now just because the people who looked down on her said so.

"They were here earlier, but they left town," she lied. "If you hurry toward the river, I bet you can catch them." The king's men took her advice, never knowing that God's spies were just a few feet away, hiding on Rahab's roof under piles of flax.

After darkness fell, Rahab uncovered them and said, "The LORD your God is the supreme God of the heavens above and the earth below" (Joshua 2:11, NLT). For a woman who'd grown up worshipping many gods, this was perhaps an even bigger betrayal to her community than lying to her king. But Rahab was now a believer. She sold out the king of Jericho because she was sold out to the King of Glory.

Knowing she was in trouble, she asked the spies for help. "Look, I hid you; now I need something. When you conquer this city, promise me you won't kill me or my family."

The spies had to be impressed with her faith. They promised if she wouldn't betray them, they'd spare her and all those who belonged to her. That night, she let them down the town wall with a scarlet rope and told the spies how to escape without being detected. The spies returned safely to their camp with valuable information for overthrowing Jericho—and an incredible story about a "fallen woman" whom God was using in mighty ways.

In opening her house to the spies, Rahab made herself over with a radical change—she showed herself willing to totally reevaluate her identity. The power of the Israelites' God changed the way she saw her life—not only her immoral profession, but also her faith and the community where she lived. The spies' love of God was irresistibly attractive to a woman who'd only ever worshipped lifeless statues.

But it wasn't all about her. Rahab wanted to spare her family, too. She'd been separated from them for a while, whether by her choice or theirs, yet she loved them so much, she negotiated for their safety.

Imagine the scene at the family's front door: "Dad, it's me, Rahab. I know it's been a few years, but you and Mom and the rest of the family need to pack your most treasured belongings and sneak over to my house without letting anyone see you."

Somehow, despite their past disagreements, she was able to persuade family members to reconcile long enough to come to her house. There the entire family huddled together while the city was taken siege and eventually overthrown. The scarlet cord that hung out of Rahab's window was the sign that her house and all who were in it should be spared. And they were.

The woman who had fallen so far, the woman considered the slut of the community, sacrificed herself and, in return, was saved. So was her family. Salmon must have watched with amazement as all of this unfolded. He knew her past, was a beneficiary of her kindness, and was a witness to her faith. His gratitude grew into something more. Eventually, he married her.

Rahab joined the family of a prince, a son of a leading family in the house of Israel. She spent the rest of her life among God's chosen people as if she were one of them.

And she was.

It was through her offspring, generations later, that Jesus was born. Rahab is one of only two foreigners and five women listed in Jesus' lineage. Her reward is great as an ancestor of the Savior.

Rahab may not have been loved by the people in her community—or at times even by her family—but God found her worthy of salvation. Despite her immoral behavior, He saw value in her even when those who knew her best didn't. God loves bad girls. Rahab is a reminder that God sees past our past, to our hearts. He can and does use anyone for His glory.

Melissa
From Princess to Freak

*W*hen four-year-old Melissa stepped into the heated baptismal waters, her white robe billowed around her stomach. *I'm a princess,* she thought. The hot white lights were blinding, preventing Melissa from seeing friends, family, and the hundreds of church members watching from the pews.

It was Melissa's spiritual rite of passage. A fairy tale that would begin with, "I baptize you in the name of..." and one day would end with, "Well done, my good and faithful servant."

But Melissa couldn't have guessed that, in a few years, this baptism wouldn't mean nearly as much to her as would a much different experience—one that would take place in cold, murky water.

Melissa was a good girl who wanted to be an actress when she grew up. In school, she studied hard and had many friends. At church, she was a role model to her peers. She memorized all the verses, preached at kids who used bad language, and tried to force conversions on all her non-Christian friends. Yes, she was *that* girl.

But Melissa's family started to move a lot, living in four states while Melissa was in elementary and middle school. By the time she entered high school, they'd come full circle, back to the small southern community where she'd started. Though the faces were familiar, Melissa found that her friends weren't. The relationships weren't easy, like before. Now they were strained and awkward. Instead of being at the center of the social circle, for the first time, Melissa was left trying to figure out how to get in at all. And her attempts often failed.

"I analyzed everything that came out of my mouth," says Melissa, whose mistakes played over and over in her mind like an iTunes playlist with only one song.

Why did I say that?

What was I thinking?

Why couldn't I do that better?

"I wanted to kick myself each time I did something stupid." She looked for ways to punish herself—doing a thousand sit-ups or skipping meals. Her self-inflicted punishments caused her to lose weight. Though Melissa had never been fat, people started noticing her figure. The attention felt good. Soon a few lost pounds became too many pounds.

Melissa had punished herself right into an eating disorder.

"It became what I knew, how I dealt with the hard stuff," says Melissa. "I didn't want to think about things, so I'd think about food, exercise, and how much I hated myself. The more my bones stuck out, the better I felt." In Melissa's mind, she had control—control she didn't have in other areas of her life.

One night at a Rebecca St. James concert, something in the music moved her. Melissa knew she needed to let others in—the eating disorder had become too big to handle on her own. After the concert, Melissa confided in her mother, hoping she'd help. Instead, her mother thought Melissa was once again being a "drama queen" and looking for attention.

Melissa *was* dramatic. But her confession wasn't an act. It was real. She needed help. And the help she sought wasn't there.

Melissa began spending less time at church and more time with the girls from school. She felt at home among the outcasts—those who were weird, even a little freaky. Their nonconformity matched her insides. She became one person at church: Good Melissa. Another at school: Freaky Melissa. And at home she was just confused. Who was the real Melissa?

Over the next few years, a pattern emerged. Good Melissa was a leader in her church. She was even a speaker at a youth evangelism conference. When things were going well, "Good Melissa" would get everything under control and the eating disorder would fade into the background.

But when she messed up, she became "Freaky Melissa." The eating disorder took control. She isolated herself from others. And she stopped going to church.

In college, things got worse. She started drinking and cutting herself. Forced into therapy, Melissa learned that she had been living with depression and borderline personality disorder. Her doctors put her on medication, which she would take until she got a handle on herself. Then, just when everyone thought things were fine, she would spiral downward again.

The week Melissa was diagnosed as bipolar, she lost her virginity in the back of a car and was kicked out of her sister's house. A few months later, she wrecked her car in an alcohol-induced blackout, spent two days in jail, and had her license taken away for a year.

It can't get any worse. I've got to stop this.

Sitting on the kitchen floor, her back pressed against the cabinets, Melissa tried to take control the only way she knew how. She took a knife from the drawer and slit her wrists.

But she didn't even do that right.

She survived, and after a trip to the ER, she spent the night in a state mental hospital. Surrounded by certifiably crazy people, Melissa knew she wasn't insane. She was desperate for a solution.

Again, Melissa picked herself up. She moved to New York to pursue her dream of being an actress. "But the pattern started again," says Melissa. She tried to stop drinking. She'd succeed for a few days or weeks, and while she was clean, she'd visit a new church. "I wanted to fit in. I wanted to connect with people. But I was afraid that if they knew my past, that would be it—they wouldn't want me in their church. So I pretended to be someone other than who I was."

A friend invited Melissa to an Alcoholics Anonymous (AA) meeting. The people all seemed so different from her. She attended for a while and then quit. Then she came back and shared a bit more. Finally, she said it: "I'm Melissa, and I'm an alcoholic."

She'd found what she was looking for—people who didn't judge her, no matter what she did. Melissa admitted defeat. "I walked into that room and asked for help from this community of drunks. At AA they like to say, 'Let us love you until you love yourself.' They loved me sober."

Melissa's sponsor told her, "If the god you have isn't working for you, get a new one." So Melissa put her Bible away, dropped out of church, and made AA her new spiritual home.

AA helped her get sober, but it didn't help her connect with God.

Melissa wanted a God who loved her as the drunks did. She wanted a God who not only accepted her but wanted her enough to chase her and knock her down with His love. And she wanted forgiveness—not only from God but from His people.

Eventually Melissa found this perfect God. His name was Jesus.

They were introduced by Jim, the pastor of a new church

in her neighborhood. Before Melissa visited Jim's church, she e-mailed him and told him everything she'd done. She warned him, "If your church can't love me unconditionally, then I'll get up and walk out."

"Not once did I see a look of surprise or disgust when I got there," says Melissa. "Instead of the legalism and rules I'd grown up with, I was encouraged to ask questions. My doubts were discussed at length. I was given love and room to explore."

On a cold October morning, Jim, his wife, and a few friends gathered to baptize Melissa in the cold, murky waters off Coney Island. The smell of corn dogs and funnel cakes drifted in the air. They heard laughter from the Ferris wheel, and if they listened closely, they could hear the barker on the Midway enticing people to "shoot the freak."

Shivering in shorts and a T-shirt, Melissa felt cold sand between her toes. She was prepared to send "Freaky Melissa" and all her sins out to sea.

"I'd been given the choice," says Melissa. "I couldn't think of a better place for my baptism than the freezing, polluted waters off Coney Island. It was everything I could have ever asked for in a baptism—dirty, disgusting, crazy Coney."

This time, Melissa was surrounded by the faces of those who had prayed for her, guided her, and—most of all—loved her unconditionally.

"I was baptized into a wave. Coming out of the water, the first thing I became aware of—as I gracefully tried to spit saltwater out of my mouth—was the sound of clapping and whoops and hollers from the beach. I remember feeling like I'd just gotten the biggest do-over in the history of do-overs. A 'get out of jail free' card—good for eternity."

Salty tears mixed with the saltwater and sand on Melissa's face. She'd never felt more loved. Or more clean.

Gwen
A Wanderer Comes Home

*G*wen's relatives pulled her aside when she was nine years old. They shared the Bible's plan of salvation, explaining to Gwen that she was a sinner deserving death, but that Jesus had taken her sins upon Himself. Terrified of hell, Gwen embraced the Gospel and became a pint-sized evangelist, sharing Jesus with all her friends.

But her unstable home life took its toll on her zeal. Gwen changed schools every year from kindergarten to fourth grade—excruciating for a shy girl who often got picked last in P.E. She spent many terrifying lunches worrying about whom she would sit with, and many evenings wondering whether her mom would again pack the family up to move in with Grandma, leaving Gwen's dad behind.

Gwen questioned whether God could protect her, or even see her. She had nightmares about hell. In her dream, a trapdoor under her bed led straight to hell, where the devil was waiting for her. She kept her dreams to herself, sure that no one would understand.

In her later elementary years, she asked herself, *If God is real, why doesn't He take care of me? And how can I trust Him? After all, He hasn't protected me.* She pictured God as a sneering judge, indifferent to her painful life. She figured He didn't like her very much, so she chose not to turn to Him anymore.

"I will live my life my way," she decided. "I know I'll do a better job, watching out for myself."

To numb her pain and cope with the challenges of moving so much (she attended four different high schools in four years), Gwen drank almost every day before school. She tried marijuana, speed, and painkillers.

Still not feeling fulfilled, Gwen had a handful of boyfriends over the years, hoping to be loved. She worried over how she looked and longed for attention from guys. She purposely dressed in sexy clothing and relished the looks that followed her. This fueled her obsession with her weight. She worked out every minute she could find, trying to achieve just the right look. "I thought I was fat," she says. "I wore a size four."

Looking back on that time, Gwen says, "I didn't really know the whole character of God. My ignorance and self-hatred made me doubt the Bible. I didn't think I could trust God with how my life was turning out. He obviously didn't care, or He thought I deserved a bad life."

Gwen moved out of the house when she was a senior, living with her best friend's family. After high school, she moved in with her boyfriend. Her life continued to spiral downward in depression. She entertained thoughts of suicide, but her grade-school fear of hell returned. She worried that if she took her own life, she'd go there. To quell the pain, Gwen let her emotions control her, alternately punching brick walls in blind rages and weeping, cradling herself in the fetal position.

She broke up with her boyfriend and dated another guy, eventually getting pregnant. Her new boyfriend told her, "Now is not the right time to have kids. We can get married and have children later." Though she knew taking the life of her child was wrong, she scheduled an abortion. During the procedure, a nurse's voice floated in and out of her mind.

"You're okay."

"It's all over."

"Here's a pad."

"Call if you have any problems."

Guilt, shame, and self-hatred flooded through her. She broke up with her boyfriend.

Gwen tried breast implant surgery to fix her insecurity, but after she felt more ashamed. "Afterward that, I felt fake outside, like I had always faked being okay inside." She partied a lot, frequenting bars with friends. During that time, she met her husband-to-be at a restaurant. They moved in together, eventually eloping to Las Vegas. They had a baby, and they ran into financial trouble.

During the first year of her marriage, Gwen was still emotionally attached to her previous boyfriend, the father of her aborted baby. She kept up her relationship with him through an emotional affair. She spent hours talking to him when she was supposed to be working. Her marriage suffered. "I couldn't stand the sight of my husband after I'd been talking to my ex-boyfriend all day," she confesses now.

"This isn't working," her husband finally said. "Are you still talking to him?"

She nodded.

"You need to call him right now. Tell him it's over."

"No, I can't. I don't love you." She told her husband to move out.

A week later, he came back, and they decided to start over. A job transfer landed them in Colorado, far from the other man. Their relationship improved, but they spent money unwisely and constantly struggled with finances. Gwen's car was repossessed. Her grandmother died, but she couldn't afford to attend her funeral.

Gwen and her husband both worked to make ends meet. Their son went to daycare at a local church, even though they were not interested in religion and did not attend. One day when she picked up her son, she realized that he had hurt himself and no one had called her. Gwen was angry and removed him from that daycare without telling any of the workers what happened. When no one from the daycare ever called to check on the status of her son, it cemented Gwen's bitterness, proving in her mind that Christians simply didn't care about people like her.

But God was still reaching out to Gwen in her complicated situation. "Life started to change when we were both offered jobs on the same day," she remembers. "And both of our bosses were believers."

Gwen wanted to change, to get past her family's rough beginning. They started by going to church together, and then started volunteering to serve together. Slowly, Gwen allowed God to remake her, body and soul.

When Gwen started to struggle with how slow the process of transformation was, God gave her a dream. "In the dream, my son had a rock tumbler. He could take the ugliest rock and put it in the tumbler, only to find it beautiful on the other end. God showed me that His purpose was to polish me like that tumbler."

The dream changed Gwen forever. "From then on, I felt that God saw me. I finally believed, and allowed God to strip me of my shame."

God has taken Gwen the Prodigal and transformed her into Gwen the Loved. "I tried men, looks, money, materialism, but nothing satisfied me. But God's love has soaked into the dry places of my soul."

Gwen, the shy girl who moved from place to place, now wants to share His love through writing and speaking. "That's another God thing," she says. "I never wanted to be a writer or a speaker, but now I can't stop talking about God and His love. He is the greatest of lovers. I am touched by His forgiveness and grace."

Lori
Picture-Perfect Paradise

*L*ori grew up in paradise, surrounded by the blue water and white beaches of the Caribbean.

But it wasn't just the place that was perfect. Lori's life, from the outside, seemed perfect, too. Her parents loved her and brought her to church. Lori can't remember the first time she asked Jesus into her heart—her mom says she was four or five. When she was ten, and old enough to really understand salvation, she prayed with a camp counselor in the rain.

Lori had lots of friends in high school and loved to babysit. Her mother homeschooled her and her sister, and the family all attended church together. On the outside, Lori lived a life that fit her "paradise" surroundings.

But behind the picture, things weren't so pretty. Lori struggled with guilt and loneliness, knowing that her heart was not as good as everyone thought it was. She wasn't doing anything wrong, exactly, but she felt badly about herself. When women told Lori that they wanted their daughters to grow up just like her, the pressure to be perfect mounted. She worried that God would see behind her mask and understand just how sinful she really was, so Lori backed away from Him. Even as she memorized verses for Sunday school and prayed with her family before meals, she felt the distance growing. She figured God didn't care.

Lori struggled with being a teenager. She was surrounded by kids her age who called themselves friends, but the relationships were shallow. No one knew who she really was. She wasn't sure they would want to—they laughed at her haircut and clothes, and she struggled to accept her weight every time she looked in a mirror. She liked a boy for years but couldn't tell him, convinced she wasn't worthy of him. Her schoolwork began to slip. Lori couldn't keep up with her academically gifted sister and started to feel like a failure in that area as well.

In fact, it was homework that pushed Lori from being silently insecure to outwardly sinful. Unable to keep up the pace, she started cheating on homework, then on tests. The guilt from this behavior intensified the pain she carried, and she started looking for ways to make it go away. She turned to what she'd heard others used when they were sad—alcohol.

Careful to keep up the perfect image, Lori drank in secret, swallowing a little bit of the gin her mother kept for Christmas baking. She didn't like the taste, though, so she went looking for something else to heal her. She tried to control how much she ate, skipping meals for a day or two at a time and throwing up when she did eat, but it was too hard to hide the effects. During those dark days, Lori started looking at explicit pictures and reading pornographic stories on the Internet, hoping to escape into fantasies where she felt better about the way she looked. Like the cheating and the insecurity before it, though, Internet pornography only grabbed on to Lori and pulled her deeper into shame and isolation. "If this is what love is," she told herself, "then I don't want it."

Lori started cutting herself with a pair of fingernail clippers. In this physical pain, she finally found some level of relief and control. She could go to church and give Sunday-school-perfect answers when people asked how she was, knowing that on her thigh, hidden by the jeans she wore all the time—even in summer—were marks and scars that showed the real her.

When she was seventeen, her family left the church she had attended all her life. The change hurt her already wounded soul. She didn't try to make friends at the new church, although she continued to go through the motions. She knew that the people in the new church were genuine and caring. She could see that her Sunday school teacher really wanted to get to know her. But she was afraid, far away from understanding the God who loved her.

It was in that Sunday school class that God finally broke through the walls of Lori's exile. Her teacher spoke one week about what it meant to shine with Christ's love, and he read a verse from 2 Corinthians:

> *"But we all, with unveiled face, beholding as in a mirror the glory of the Lord, are being transformed into the same image from glory to glory, just as by the Spirit of the Lord."* (2 CORINTHIANS 3:18, NASB)

It was a shocking moment for Lori, to hear and really understand for the first time that God wanted to see her—all of her—without the veil of picture-perfect behavior. Lori had been looking in mirrors for years, seeing nothing but ugliness. Now, with Paul's words to the church in Corinth echoing in her mind, she knew she had to let God, and the people around her, see her clearly.

That day, before she left church, she told her parents, "I'm telling you now before I back down—there are things we need to talk about today." When they got home, Lori laid out the cheating and the drinking. Her parents were shocked, but supportive. They had always seen Lori the way God saw her, as a beautiful young woman. Although her words hurt them, they were glad to know what was really going on and committed to praying for their daughter as she sought the peace of a God who really, truly loved her.

The change wasn't immediate. Lori still struggled with the temptations of her past behavior. A few months after she talked to her parents, she found herself in the bathroom with the nail clippers. *Just a few marks,* she thought. But instead of the straight lines she'd always cut, she found herself cutting a word—LOVE—into her leg. And as she looked at the ugly marks and the beautiful word, God's love finally broke through her heart as well as her head. She knew at that moment that she was loved. Not because she branded herself—that was a mistake. But because God had sent His Son, who was branded in ways more horrible than what she could do in her own home.

Today, Lori strives to be transparent with those around her. She is on her way to a Bible college, determined to start her life fresh and to rest in the secure love of Christ. She knows she was rescued by a power far greater than her own. "I'd clearly still be in a pit today if God hadn't taken me from all I'd ever known and made me completely rely on Him and start my life from scratch," she says.

Linda
Accepted

For Linda, it wasn't as if, all of a sudden, lightning struck and she became a Christian. She grew up around Christians, in a home filled with Christian traditions. Her grandparents were missionaries in Asia for over thirty years. She accepted Christ as her Savior and was baptized when she was seven, although that was mostly because only baptized church members got to drink the grape juice on Communion Sundays.

Linda followed along and did the "Christian thing" for years: getting involved in church activities, memorizing Scripture, and more. By high school, though, her Christian-culture lifestyle was starting to feel like a mask that didn't fit well. She was tired and wanted to act more like other kids her age.

The changes started gradually. Linda wanted to be seen as an individual and resented her father's strict rules. They started fighting. "I wanted to do things to make my parents mad and get back at them for how frustrated they were making me. Every time I got into trouble, Dad preached at me, so it made me resent my parents, then God, and, ultimately, the church."

Guys and alcohol were Linda's weaknesses. When she was fourteen, Linda visited relatives in another state, where she met the daughter of a family friend. The girl, who was about her age, mentioned a party that was happening that night.

The party was in a dangerous neighborhood, no place for two fourteen-year-old girls. The people at the party were all strangers, all older, and all much rougher than anyone Linda knew. That night, Linda was drugged and raped by a man she had never seen before and would never see again.

"After that, I was angry. A lot." Linda remembers now. Her anger turned quickly to bitterness toward her parents. They had found out about the party through the family friends, but Linda thought the story had been twisted to make it seem like it was all her idea. She didn't think her parents believed her version of what happened, and she struggled with the weight of their judgment and her own guilt. She always knew that what had happened was due to her own poor judgment. "I could have said, 'No, I don't want to go,' but I didn't. I wanted to party with the cool kids. And God protected me even in my poor choices. The guy could have killed me that night."

Linda's guilt began to push her toward a deep depression. She started cutting herself and sleeping around to distract herself from the pain she felt inside.

"I would take a knife, or sometimes scissors or nail clippers, and cut my thighs and upper arms, areas that people couldn't really see. My legs were the part of my physical appearance I hated most." Linda still has scars on her forearms and wrists that she kept covered with long sleeves and bracelets for a long time.

Cutting provided some relief from the hurt inside, but it only lasted for a few minutes. The emotional pain came flooding back with even more intensity than before, as soon as the physical pain was gone.

She experimented with some over-the-counter drugs, even

getting kicked out of Bible camp for abusing the over-the-counter stimulant NoDoz, but she never used any illegal substances. She explains, "I was always searching for some reason to stay alive. I had suicidal thoughts, but never once did I actually think I was going to kill myself, because deep down I knew there was some reason I was still here." That same desire to live kept her from going down much darker paths.

Linda remained involved in church activities throughout her rebellion. "Christian stuff" provided some sort of safety net, though she was still closing her heart to God.

After Linda graduated from high school, her parents sent her to work at the Asian orphanage with her grandparents for a few months. Linda's heart began to soften as she witnessed God's miraculous provision for the orphanage and the union of Christian couples with their newly adopted children. She returned home on her eighteenth birthday, humbled and aware that she needed someone to depend on who was always going to be there—and that Person was God.

Linda's faith was not yet stronger than her temptations. Her friends were gone, so she moved to a new city where she could figure things out for herself. A job opportunity fell through and she ended up working at a restaurant for a few months, partying some with the other wait staff. But her feelings of deep loneliness hovered, and her experiences at the orphanage never left her mind. With no other solutions, Linda started praying and having daily devotions. This new city, with its parties and lack of accountability, was not where God wanted her to be. Linda returned home.

Three weeks later, she ran into Aidan, a faithful Christian friend she had known growing up. They started dating, and three months later, Aidan asked her to commit to pray about their relationship. She agreed, and for twelve days they prayed, together and alone. "We had no physical contact, not even holding hands, during that time … We wanted no distractions so we could hear God's voice." It was an entirely new experience for Linda.

Aidan proposed a week later, and the couple married three months after that.

It hasn't been an easy transition for Linda. The scars that remain from that dark night at the party have caused Linda psychological trauma at times, and her past mistakes affect their relationship. "One of the hardest things was my wedding night. I was his first [sexual partner], but I couldn't say the same about him."

Linda is blessed with a strong family life, and she now has a restored relationship with her parents. Her family's support and unconditional love have also strengthened her through the difficult days. Through sharing the pain of the past, Linda and Aidan, together, know what it means to offer grace to one another. "He accepted me just as I was … He accepted me." She could not ask for a better example of Christ's love.

Elise
Released from the Cage

*T*he amazing thing about grace," says Elise, "is that you don't have to be perfect. That's the whole point. God knows and loves us as we are and says He can still use us even so. I think that, for a long time, I've thought I need to get my act together before God can ever love me, embrace me, and call me His daughter. What rot! What lies!"

Elise's story is a series of beautiful and painful images. When she was seven, she was hit by a car, injured badly and lucky to have survived. God used that injury, though, to bring her to the church where she first began to understand the love of God. At fourteen, Elise prayed at a youth event to accept Christ. "I still didn't totally understand about the Cross or the Holy Spirit," she says, "but what I did know was that there was an ache in my life, a hole, and Jesus wanted me—little old me. I came home that night with a smile a foot wide and a desire to really follow Jesus."

Elise became the quintessential teenager, trying to fit in. She liked church, and she liked music, and hanging out with friends, and drinking and smoking—and her world started to split. She wanted so much to be loved and accepted, but felt like her parents' love was conditional, based on her behavior. So Elise turned to boys. "I thought, early on, that sex was a trade-off with men. They give you hugs and kisses and tell you you're special, and you give them sex in return."

For a long time Elise struggled between two worlds. She married someone out of fear of being alone. He became a Christian, and they tried to pray together, tried to make it work, but it was a constant struggle. He was jealous and insecure; their arguments could become violent. Their church didn't know how to help them.

And Elise kept making bad choices. She had an affair and got pregnant. Not knowing what else to do, and not wanting to confess to her husband, she had an abortion. The father of the baby did not know how to comfort her. In spite of an initial sense of relief, Elise became immersed in self-hatred. "My life was over, devastated by my own actions. No one could condemn me more than I did myself."

So Elise ran, further and further. She and her husband divorced. She drank and did drugs—ecstasy, cocaine—trying to numb herself from the pain of all the mistakes she had made. She considered taking her own life. God was still present, but only as a distant image—as a parent or policeman, someone who was constantly disappointed in her, constantly thinking she should be doing better.

But in the midst of the darkness, her loving Father God began planting other images—images of hope and healing. Soon after the abortion, Elise caught a horrible case of bronchitis, requiring her to rest for two weeks. "I cried out, and God gave me a vision of myself laid out flat in His throne room, sensing His holiness and being very afraid. Then I saw the hand of Jesus, pierced and bloody, reach out to touch me in a comforting way, and I knew I wouldn't be struck down, because He was taking care of me, standing up for me."

During the time when Elise's marriage was falling apart, she attended church with some good friends. The pastor presented the image of a woman in a cage, crying and distraught, feeling trapped. The cage door was open, but she had her back to the door, so she couldn't see the way out. "I knew it was me," she says. "I knew all I had to do was reach out to God, beg for forgiveness, and come home, but I didn't. I was torn between God and a man. So that image captured so perfectly my state of being. Here I was—hurt, discouraged, distressed, and angry—yet knowing the cure for all of that and still not reaching out to the one Person who could help me." Elise broke down in tears.

A Sunday school teacher from the church she had attended as a child gave Elise another picture of her life: "She said she saw me as a boat tied to the harbor wall. The tide would pull me away from the dock, but the rope always held me there. At other times, I would drift to the wall under my own momentum. The rope was Jesus Christ, never letting me get away from Him completely."

Jesus did not let her get away, but found countless ways to comfort her. He gave Elise friends she couldn't have lived without. They put their arms around her, prayed with her, spoke words of encouragement. One day when she was struggling with suicidal thoughts, a dear friend walked to Elise's house over her lunch break to give her a verse, Psalm 118:17: "I will not die; instead, I will live to tell what the Lord has done" (NLT). God was giving Elise images of life—through friends and through nature and music. "I would see a sunset and be filled with the knowledge that God had made it and it really was good. That singular thought would lead me on a pathway back to Him."

Over the years, Elise's life transitioned from one of hopelessness to one full of hope and forgiveness. It was the love of

God that brought Elise home. She is still on her journey, but she knows she walks in the comforting arms of her Father.

The image that embodies her life today is that of the prodigal son—or daughter, in her case. "I am still on the journey home, but my Father has run up the road and hugged me. We're walking together back to the house—as I stink up the vicinity. I lean into Him and He holds me close, stroking my hair and telling me that He loves me, over and over again."

Today Elise shares her story, through her blog and through poetry, to help others with their journey back to God and His immense love. Elise was led away by her insecurity, her fears, her desire to be loved—and by anger and guilt. She was brought home by a deep understanding of God's unconditional love. "God loves all of us so much—He sent His Son to die a horrific death for us. He longs to have a relationship with us, not just have us do good things. Everything stems from that. I don't think I understood that at the beginning."

Taylor
Beauty from Ashes

I don't like you right now," Taylor's mom told her, pain in her eyes.

"I don't like myself," seventeen-year-old Taylor responded. And she meant it.

Several months earlier, her boyfriend had pressured her into having sex. On the way home, she cried, believing she was "ruined." She figured once she'd "done it," she couldn't start over, so she continued sleeping around, losing bits and pieces of her soul in the process. Although she had met Jesus when she was twelve, the condemning voices in her head screamed louder than His gentle love and forgiveness.

"At that point in my life, I mentally ran away. I separated myself from my parents emotionally. I withdrew. I kept everything inside, not telling a soul."

In college she started dating a boy who seemed to adore her. They were inseparable until unexpectedly he broke up with her without explanation. Not long after, she went to his apartment unannounced and found him with another girl. Devastated, she talked through the night with his best friend. They drank too much. They ended up having sex, and soon after, she found out she was pregnant.

"I decided to have an abortion. I didn't know about those verses in the Bible that say God knows babies in the womb before they were born. The media convinced me it was a fetus, not a baby. I didn't stop long enough to think through the decision. I was simply motivated by fear—fear that I wouldn't be able to finish college, and fear that my parents would then know I was sexually active. In my mind, abortion was a viable form of birth control," Taylor says.

One of her friends tried to persuade Taylor to keep the baby. "You and I can raise the baby together," her girlfriend pleaded.

But Taylor had a more powerful voice in her head. The longer she waited, the louder it would get.

The father of the baby drove her to the abortion clinic. "I remember deliberately giving my real name. I worried that if I gave a fake name and something went wrong, no one would be able to find me." After the abortion, Taylor spent several lonely days in the house of some acquaintances who were out of town so she could recover without anyone knowing.

"I felt like the blackest, darkest cloud descended on me," she says. "Yet God must've been there, because I didn't kill myself." She slept for four solid days.

Slowly, painfully, she started realizing what she'd done. But she didn't know what to do with her grief. Just as she did after high school, she again pulled away, kept to herself.

She went back to church, but Taylor knew she didn't belong. Wracked by guilt over the abortion, the shame had strange ways of lynching her, and most often, it reared its head in church. Although she liked the pastor's laid-back ways, she avoided church whenever his son preached, because he was loud and seemed angry.

Not long after, she was driving and flipping through radio stations when she heard the pastor's son's voice blare. She stopped the dial, shocked to hear him.

His voice pitched, "Have you ever felt so bad about something you did that you go to God and keep saying, 'Please forgive me; please forgive me; please forgive me'?"

Taylor nodded.

His voice swelled. "How dare you ask over and over for God to forgive you! If you can't forgive yourself, you're making yourself out to be bigger than God. Isn't what Jesus did on the cross *enough*? How *dare* you!"

In that moment, tears streaming down her face, Taylor chose to believe that God had forgiven her. She made a decision: she wasn't going to have sex until marriage. "I was going to be the Christian I thought I was supposed to be."

The next guy she dated, she told up front, "I've had an abortion, and I'm not going to have sex until after marriage." He loved her where she was, and soon they were engaged.

And yet, the grief of the abortion lingered. On her wedding day, as she stood arm-in-arm with her father in the back of the church, she heard a baby crying. All she could think about was her own choice to end the life of her first child. Then, when it took longer than expected to get pregnant, she feared God was punishing her. Even after having two children, she still held on to the shame.

Taylor experienced a breakthrough during a demonstration at church, where a woman potter talked about creating clay pots and explained the Bible story found in Jeremiah 18:3–4: "So I went down to the potter's house, and I saw him working at the wheel. But the pot he was shaping from the clay was marred in his hands; so the potter formed it into another pot, shaping it as seemed best to him" (NIV).

"If a crack formed, the only thing for the potter to do was to throw the clay back on the wheel and start again. That's what Jesus wants for you. He has remade you. You are new," the woman said.

Taylor sat in church, stunned. She'd made the decision to start anew after hearing the preacher's voice in the car, but this was the first time she'd thought about how God had completely remade her in that moment. He could no longer see the old Taylor. She was brand-new.

Still, the shame lingered, overpowering Taylor's fragile sense of forgiveness. When the doctor wanted to test some possibly cancerous tumors in her uterus, she concluded that God would take her life, and that she deserved it. Standing in the kitchen, tears wetting her face, she begged God, "Please don't let me die. Please, God. Please let me see my children's children."

The doorbell rang. A delivery person handed Taylor a package. She unwrapped it. Inside was a gift from her sister-in-law—a beautiful handmade platter in her favorite colors. She called her sister-in-law. "What is this for?" she asked.

"It's a gift I bought for you, but it's from God." Her sister-in-law explained that she'd been on a retreat where a lady potter gave a demonstration and explained a Bible verse. Afterward, folks could buy her pottery, but the platter she knew Taylor would like was very expensive. "I couldn't go to sleep. I argued with God about it. He said, 'I provide all your needs. Buy that one for Taylor.'"

Taylor listened, tears in her eyes. "Do you know why God told you to buy that?"

"No."

Taylor, who'd only told her husband about the abortion, shared the whole story. "God knew I needed to be reminded today that He's not taking my life. I am His new creation. He does not condemn His new creations."

The stoneware is symbolic on many levels. From a black background emerge two clusters of grapes. "Out of the darkness, God's given me two children," Taylor says.

Yet God still had more tangible surprises of healing in store. At a women's retreat, Taylor won a centerpiece—in the same colors as the platter—and ended up attending the workshop represented by the centerpiece. The speaker talked about how important it was to tell others your story. Taylor wept through the presentation, aware that she had an amazing story to tell but couldn't bring herself to tell it. She talked with the presenter, who encouraged her to go through an abortion recovery Bible study. At the end of the twelve-week Bible study, the participants held a funeral for their aborted babies.

The hardest part of Taylor's journey was deciding to tell her story to her parents. For weeks, she wrestled with God. He told her, "If you've trusted Me with your heart, why can't you trust Me with your parents' hearts?"

The meeting was excruciating—lots of tears. But the Lord held her parents tenderly as Taylor unfolded her prodigal story. The next day her mother took her to lunch. "On my hands and knees, I have begged God to reveal to me why you had a wall up between us, why there was a disconnect between us." She looked Taylor in the eyes and said, "Welcome home."

Annette
Casting Every Care

Six-year-old Annette watched her Sunday school teacher press a black heart to a felt board during Sunday school. "Because of our sins, our hearts are black," she said. She pulled out a white heart. "Jesus died on the cross for our sins. If we ask Him to come into our hearts, He will make them pure white." Annette longed for that white heart, so she gave hers to Jesus.

Annette matured early, wearing training bras in third grade, starting her period in fourth. Classmates teased her, making fun of her acne and her size. "I desperately wanted to feel loved and valued just as I was, and I never did. Instead, I sought the affections of boys, even in elementary school."

Annette's father tried to encourage her, but she heard his words as more criticism of her weight and skin. Lost in her own insecurity, she did not feel loved or valued by him. "No one was speaking truth into my life. No one said, 'You're beautiful. You're fine. You just grew up fast.'"

She traveled down the prodigal path from seventh grade until she graduated from college. She started drinking in seventh grade, joining a circle of partying friends. That year, she lost her virginity, and her good reputation. "I had been a leader among my classmates, but by junior high, the choices I was making caused people to think I was a slut. I felt miserable, even suicidal, and I didn't tell anyone how I felt." She continued a dizzying cycle of alcohol and sex throughout junior high and high school. Sometimes she'd stop having sex because she felt awful about herself, but she'd always go back to sexual activity. Later, she met a boy she fell in love with, but their abrupt breakup devastated her. She drank half a bottle of rum to numb her pain.

Annette attended church camp after she graduated from high school. Though her heart had been hardened toward her faith for years, the counselor's words sunk in and she gave her life back to Jesus by week's end. "I knew the choices I had been making had brought me to this awful place, and I knew He was the way out of it."

Unfortunately, like many prodigals Annette overestimated her ability to withstand peer pressure. "The first time I was faced with drinking, I succumbed. The guilt was overwhelming. I felt completely unworthy, so instead of confessing, I spiraled downward again."

Annette attended a Christian college and lived with a Christian roommate from her hometown. Even so, she quickly found a group of party-minded friends and turned her back on Christ. "I felt free," she says, "and wanted nothing to do with church or Jesus."

She continued pursuing guys, often blaming them for her relational turmoil. Friends introduced her to recreational drugs—ecstasy, LSD, mushrooms, cocaine. She enjoyed marijuana so much that by her sophomore year, she smoked it almost daily.

"By the end of my sophomore year and all through my junior year, I began to feel like things were moving in the right direction," Annette says. "I felt in control of my grades. I felt in control of my work. I felt in control of my partying. I felt in control of my interaction with guys. Then the bottom fell out when my parents split up because my dad had been having an affair."

The shock of her parents' separation sent Annette spiraling. She doused her pain with sex, alcohol, and drugs. Eventually she realized she needed a change of pace. She broke up with her boyfriend and decided to move to another state for a summer. Before she left, she met with her former pastor, spilling her story. He told her she shouldn't expect to be instantly better, that it had taken a long time for her to get where she was and it would take a long time to fight her way back.

In her new home, she led a double life, befriending Christians and attending Bible studies, but partying on the side. When she returned to college for her senior year, she jumped into her old life: partying, sleeping around, smoking pot.

That fall, she found out her best friend from childhood, who had been with her through every trial, had betrayed her. Devastated by yet another blow to her fragile self-esteem, Annette called everyone she could think of, but no one answered their phones. "I was crying and praying and asking God to let someone answer. I was sick of my life."

Finally, Annette's roommate from her freshman year answered the phone and invited her to come over. Annette told the girl about everything—the partying, the drugs, and the sex. "I felt like the weight of the world had been lifted off me," she says. At her friend's urging, Annette went home intending to throw away all of the drugs and paraphernalia still in her apartment, buoyed by knowing that her friend was praying for her while she was doing it.

But before she could do anything, Annette sat on her bed and began to read a book filled with God's promises. She wondered if it was all true. Could she cast every care on Jesus? Was His yoke light? She realized she'd bought into the lie that it was a drag to be a Christian.

Annette got on her knees. "With tears streaming down my face, I confessed it all to Him—every sordid detail. I asked Him to forgive me, and at that moment, felt totally clean, like I had the pure white heart my Sunday school teacher had shown me all those years ago." She felt like her dim room became very bright, and in that moment, God completely wrapped her in His arms. She lay on the floor. "I couldn't get low enough," she says.

She gathered all her drugs, shoving them into a paper sack and depositing them in the trash can outside. She changed her phone number and cut off communication with her former friends. She attended Bible studies. Though she was alone, she never felt lonely. "Even though I had accepted Jesus as my Savior at six years old, I came to realize that I didn't let Him be Lord and King until I was twenty."

In retrospect, Annette thinks her struggle with being loved fueled her rebellion. "I didn't believe I was loved unconditionally and that, no matter what the world said, I was captivating and beautiful to my heavenly Father. I based my worth on my performance, and when I didn't perform well, my thoughts about who I was and what I believed were tainted. I returned to Christ when I came to the end of myself and realized that love and acceptance could only be found in Jesus."

Today Annette is a successful businesswoman, happily married with three children. The hardest part of her prodigal journey has been handling her regret. "It is a challenge to choose not to be consumed by shame and guilt and live life in response to that." But God has been gracious to her along the journey, replacing her childhood insecurities with a genuine belief that God has chosen her to be His own. Knowing she is beloved by God smoothes away the edges of the past, keeping her hopeful in the present and joyful about the future.

part two

Addictions

In the beginning…

Gomer

She was a girl from the wrong side of the camel tracks. When you come from a place like that, during a time like that, no one keeps formal records. Facts are hard to come by, but rumors trashing Gomer's reputation continue to flow like cheap wine at a wedding.

Gomer came from a pagan family, very different from the God-fearing community where she ended up. Her husband's people must have whispered about her past life, pretending to be shocked by the "free love" behavior of Gomer's relatives. There were accusations about perverse acts and sexual orgies as part of the idol worship. There were immature snickers that Gomer's father's name was a word that meant "sensuous."

People probably believed the worst about Gomer even before she gave them any reason to. She was tainted with the stains of her family's reputation.

But it seems that Gomer had tried to put the unhealthy behaviors behind her and move past the ways her family lived. She married a good man—a decent, hardworking, religious Jew named Hosea, who was held in high esteem as a prophet—a man who heard God speak and acted on what he heard. Hosea's job was to share with the religious community what God wanted them to do or to know. Hosea loved his job, and he loved his God. But Gomer was never sure—did he love her?

The Bible says that Hosea married Gomer because God

told him to, and Hosea did whatever God said. This must have confused Gomer. Why did this man want her? Did he even want her?

When Gomer and Hosea got married, it seems that Hosea didn't know about her past or her family's behavior. He didn't ask what she had seen growing up, and didn't seem to consider how those experiences would affect her as an adult. Psychology and therapy were still centuries away.

But that didn't mean the neighbors didn't know.

"What's she doing with a guy like that?"

"I guess he married her for *one* thing," would come the reply, and then they'd laugh.

Gomer must have heard them. Whether she was guilty of the sins, or a sinner by association with her family, it didn't matter. Gomer felt judged and sentenced to a punishment she couldn't escape.

In the middle of the pressure, it must have been hard for Gomer to fight the pull to return to her old way of life—a life where physical pleasure was immediate, and where people didn't judge each other.

Gomer tried to do the right thing. She tried to fit in. She and Hosea had three kids. But it didn't help; the neighbors just had more to talk about. When taking the kids for a walk, she could hear their whispers: "Those aren't his kids; they don't even look like him."

Whether she'd been sexually active before she got married or not, Gomer couldn't get past the things she'd been exposed to growing up. She craved the touch of many men, the excitement of parties. Her thoughts were obsessive. She wanted to feel like someone loved her and wanted her for her own sake. Gomer spent less time thinking about her husband and more time thinking about herself. She was addicted to attention, money, and most of all, sex.

We don't know all the details of how it happened, but Gomer definitely walked away from her wedding vows. Men paid her for her time. She got high on the experience. She bragged about the money she earned prostituting herself. It wasn't a secret; she flaunted her actions and used her tainted money to build gardens and fountains.

Hosea was angry. He threatened to take her to court. He refused to be her husband, and he told her she was dressing like a whore. More than once he threatened to leave.

But in the end, it was Gomer who left. She may have convinced herself that Hosea's anger meant he'd never loved her. Or perhaps she was so far gone into her addictions that she didn't need to justify her sin. She left her husband for men who wined and dined her. Men who gave her nice clothes, perfume, and jewelry. Gomer abandoned her husband and three kids to pursue the highs that sex gave her.

Gomer was the first sex addict in the Bible.

And she did what many addicts do. She gave up everything to chase the temporary good feelings of her addiction. She left her husband, her kids, and even her self-respect to pursue her cravings.

Hosea was devastated. He may have been angry at her behavior before, but after Gomer left he was simply heartbroken. Hosea may have married her because God told him to, but he'd fallen in love with his wife. Hosea sat in front of his house day after day and cried out to God. And the Bible says that God came and mourned with him.

"Now you know what it feels like to be me," God told His prophet. Because the Father, too, loved Gomer, and felt the bitter emptiness of her absence when she chose to walk away.

Time passed. The Bible doesn't tell us how long, but it was enough for the high of Gomer's addiction to wear off. And then God told Hosea to go get Gomer and bring her back. God knew that the prodigal daughter had fallen too far and needed help to make her way back to the holy path. And He knew that Hosea loved his wife—and loved his God—enough to swallow his pride and reach out.

Hosea found Gomer in the heart of the city, a slave not only to her addictions but to the pagan temple itself. Alone, without security and protection, without religion and comfort, godless and prayerless, she was so indebted to those who helped satisfy her lusts that she was no longer free to leave. The initial high was gone. Only the pain remained. Gomer had hit bottom.

When Hosea walked in, we don't know if Gomer felt hopeful or ashamed. Perhaps she experienced both—shame to be seen in the state she was in, yet hope that somehow this man, this good man who worshipped purely and without sin, might be able to help her.

Hosea, with God's guidance, did the unimaginable. He bought back his wife, who had sold herself into the slavery of her addictions. With one redemptive act, Hosea set Gomer free from her past, free from bondage. And in that action, God's love released Gomer's heart, as well. For the first time, she was free of her past and her temptations.

Gomer found the strength to come clean. She went home with Hosea. And though the neighbors still talked—almost three thousand years later, they're still talking about her—the Bible indicates that Gomer re-entered Jewish society with the knowledge that she was truly loved, and lived the rest of her life as Hosea's wife, loved by God and saved from the temptations she had once thought were undeniable.

Lynn
A Desire to Do Good

*L*ynn's story reflects what many young women go through—a roller coaster of trying and failing and then trying again. Lynn grew up going to church and learning about God, but she says that during her difficult teenage years, God was not a part of her life. She smoked pot for the first time when she was twelve, and things went downhill quickly. She ran away from home at thirteen and fourteen. "I loved the thrill of running," she says in a video interview made when she was twenty-one. "I never thought anything through.... If I wanted to do something, I did it. I didn't think about the consequences."

Over and over, Lynn's parents prayed with her, and she expressed her desire to get away from the "wrong crowd" and live a better life. When she was fifteen, she changed schools three times, always hoping to get away from the bad influences and the drugs that continued to drag her down dangerous paths. But wherever she went, Lynn found herself attracted to people who hurt her. Finally, she agreed to make a dramatic clean break and voluntarily enrolled in an out-of-state Christian program for troubled teens, where she could clear her head and seek God under careful supervision. She came home still confused, still tempted, but God was faithful to give her a chance.

Rather than return to the temptations of her high school friends, Lynn got her GED and enrolled in college at sixteen. For a few months, her desire to do good overcame the temptations Satan threw in her path.

But eventually the wrong crowd caught up to Lynn again. She moved out of her parents' house at seventeen and got her own apartment. She had a car, a job, a place to live—"everything I ever wanted when I was a teenager and thought about the ideal life." Lynn reveled in the freedom of her independence. But with the independence came more mistakes. She let a few friends back into her life and got hooked on drugs again. Eventually, she was evicted. Broke and with nowhere to go, Lynn faced a choice: she could go back and live with her parents, or she could find another way forward. She had no idea what she wanted to do with her life. After so many years of trials, she felt as if she had failed at everything. And so, in a rash decision, she decided to join the Army.

In hindsight, she knows that that choice didn't make sense. She had always struggled with authority and hated being told what to do. An organization fundamentally based on discipline and submission was not a good fit for her.

Lynn's military experience was doomed almost from the start. On her first leave, she smoked pot and failed a drug test when she returned to base. She hoped that that would be the end of her military career—"that they would just kick me out and get it over with." Instead, the Army put her on restriction and docked her pay. Lynn, perhaps subconsciously, decided to try again. She ran away, going AWOL (absent without leave) and diving back into the world of drugs. She developed a strong addiction to cocaine. She couldn't afford the drugs her body demanded, so she started stealing to support her habit. She took credit cards and checkbooks, anything she could get her hands on. And when she was finally arrested for shoplifting, it all caught up with her.

A military court sentenced Lynn to three years in a military prison for theft and drug use. She was sent thousands of miles from her family and any friends she had left, and locked up with sixty other women. She was nineteen, scared, and alone.

In solitary confinement, all Lynn had to read was a Bible. And in those long hours, God revealed Himself to her. With all her defenses shattered, all her options taken away, Lynn surrendered her desires. "The emptiness went away," Lynn says on a video made the day she was released from prison. "I felt so complete. It was something I had been searching for all my life. And it was always right in front of my face, but I never grabbed hold of it. I finally did, and I would never give it up for anything. I don't need anything else."

During the time Lynn spent in prison, she sought God every day. She played guitar in the worship band and reached out to the other inmates, rejoicing when they responded to altar calls. When she was released, she seemed to be the prodigal returning home at long last.

But Lynn's story doesn't end there. While she tried to stay focused on the good and pursue God, she made mistakes. In a letter written two years after her release, she says, "I see where I went wrong. I put all my focus on getting re-established and being 'successful' in society, and little focus on continuing to grow spiritually. I slowly veered off God's path. It wasn't intentional; I think it rarely is. But once I got off that straight and narrow just a tiny bit, over time I became far away without realizing it."

Lynn started doing drugs again and failed a drug test that was part of her parole requirements. On her last day of parole, when she thought she was going to pick up her completion certificate, she was arrested and taken back to prison. She served another month.

Again, Lynn believed she had learned her lesson. But Satan knew her weaknesses and how to trap her. A friend needed her help, so she agreed to stay with him. He dragged her right back into a life of addiction. Lynn was evicted from her apartment again, lost her job, and sold all her possessions before God brought her to complete brokenness and she cried out to Him.

The pattern has been repeated several times since then. Addiction follows her. Today, Lynn is hesitant to tell her story. "I don't understand myself," she says, and quotes Paul's statement in Romans 7: *"For I have the desire to do what is good, but I cannot carry it out. For what I do is not the good I want to do; no, the evil I do not want to do—this I keep on doing."* (NIV)

Yet she believes there is always hope. "It's really been an incredible journey," she writes in a letter. "When I look back on my life and think about all the trials I've been through, one thing has remained constant: God has NEVER left my side.... He always takes me back!"

And that, after all, is the message of the prodigal. Jesus' story in Luke 15 is a powerful reminder of a father's forgiveness. We rejoice with the family when the son comes home and the party is under way. But in real life, the prodigal's return is often only the beginning. The only thing in life that never changes is God. He forgives over and over and over again. He always loves, and is always standing there, waiting for the moment we are most broken and ready to accept Him.

Melanie
Sweet Surrender

By anyone's standards, sixteen-year-old Melanie's life was out of control. She was locked in the mental ward of a hospital, where the emergency room crisis counselor had sent her after she'd threatened to kill her parents. It was either that or jail, so an unrepentant Melanie allowed herself to be committed, hoping to score enough prescription medicine to continue her lifestyle of addiction.

Things had spiraled downward for a year, ever since Melanie made what she now calls "the worst decision of my life." One night, the adopted daughter of a pastor got drunk and tried drugs for the first time. And in that self-destructive act, Melanie found a few hours of escape from the emotional issues that plagued her.

Melanie never felt like she fit in. Making friends seemed harder for her than for other kids. Emotions controlled her; she was hyper one minute and viciously angry the next. Rejection crushed her, whether it came from an elementary school playmate or from a God she thought didn't make her "good enough" to live up to her own expectations. She was a mistake, she thought, and after a distant cousin committed suicide, she became obsessed with thoughts of death and dying, believing that she wasn't worthy to live.

In eighth grade, Melanie met a group of kids who welcomed her and made her feel like part of a clique. She didn't care that they used drugs and even sold them. When they invited her to a party, she went along, ready to try whatever they gave her.

Three months after her first experience with marijuana, Melanie was a mess. She did some kind of drug every day, from pot to pills to whatever she could find in the medicine cabinet. Getting high took over her life; she craved the next experience before her current high had even worn off. She sold drugs and her own body to pay for her habit. "I couldn't go to sleep at night without drugs. I couldn't stay awake without drugs. I couldn't do anything without drugs. I was trying to hide so much and mask so much pain through partying. It was all so tiring," she remembers now.

Thoughts of death continued to plague her, and Melanie's choices often put her life at risk. One day she skipped school, got high, and went for a drive. She was in a serious head-on car accident, and was so badly injured that she had to be taken to the hospital in a helicopter. After a long, painful recovery, Melanie came home even more addicted to narcotics than before. She went right back to skipping school and driving under the influence.

After the accident, Melanie's wild behavior rapidly outpaced even that of her drug-dealing friends. When she was drunk or high, her anger poured out and she would cry for hours, threatening to kill herself and anyone around her. She started to fantasize about killing other people as well as herself, and found escape in the horrible images that filled her mind.

Finally, Melanie's parents took action. They overheard her talking on the phone about her death wishes and how she wanted to "slaughter" them. Frightened and overwhelmed, they confronted her, but she pushed them away in a rage. She dared them to call the police and report what they'd heard. Instead, Melanie's parents took her to the emergency room and then to the mental ward. She fought back the entire time and counted the days and hours until she could go back to her drug-fueled life.

But Melanie's parents wouldn't let her continue her self-destruction. When they picked her up from the hospital, they told her she wouldn't be coming home. Instead, she would travel halfway across the country to a residential program for troubled girls. It was a last-ditch effort to help Melanie get her life together.

Through intense counseling and outdoor activity, Melanie's counselors tried to guide her toward spiritual and physical healing. The days were long, full of group activities, chores, school, and personal therapy. It was a dramatic difference from Melanie's self-destructive suburban lifestyle. And though she didn't know it right away, it was exactly what she needed.

For the first five months, Melanie refused to let the concern of the center's staff touch her damaged soul. She dreamed about her old life and lashed out at everyone. Physical withdrawal from drugs was nothing compared to her deep sense of self-hatred that manifested in homicidal rage.

But God removed Melanie from her old vices and escapes for a reason. The structure of the program and the constant examples of God's love carved new channels into her soul. And one night, after a long day of physical work and an unwelcome run up the hill to her cabin, Melanie collapsed physically and emotionally. She remembers what happened next:

"I was furious [about having to run], and I was thinking how dumb I was for getting so furious over running, and I hated myself for it. So I was running and crying and thinking about so much stuff... and when I got to the top [of the hill]

I just couldn't do it anymore. I couldn't keep up with so much hate, and I broke down. I decided that maybe everyone there was right and God was the only way. Maybe I should stop shunning Him and give Him a chance."

Melanie lay on the ground outside her cabin, and for the first time since her life started to spiral out of control, she prayed. Over and over she cried out, "I'm sorry" as she laid her past behavior and mistakes at Jesus' feet. As burdens were lifted, Melanie's head came up off the ground and she decided to take a step toward healing. After fighting her counselors for months and her parents for years, Melanie decided to try things their way.

For the next thirteen months in the program, Melanie committed to tell the truth more often and to listen better. She opened up to her therapist and took her assignments for spiritual growth and healing seriously. It wasn't an overnight change—she still struggled with anger and lashed out without warning. But over time, God worked on her soul. Her hate was replaced by His love, and by the time she graduated, she could hold her head up and announce that she was loved.

"God has completely forgiven me," she reports with a smile. "I never thought it was possible. But I learned about who God truly is, and I learned how to repent. The first time I ever felt God's forgiveness, I could have been the happiest person in the world. I felt so much joy and peace, I could barely contain myself. It felt like heaven on earth."

Today, Melanie is living with her parents again, working toward becoming a veterinarian and volunteering for her church. Her life is completely changed, a testimony to what God can do even when things seem out of control.

Rose
Finding Sure Footing

*A*s a child, Rose loved to be outdoors; she and her best friend would play in the meadows and fields behind where the girls lived. The beautiful rolling hills were full of sheep and the shepherds who cared for them. Rose loved to watch the sheep graze as the sheepherders ensured their safety.

But one shepherd became too interested in the girls. He molested them and told them that if they told anyone, they would be in trouble. The crime happened in the 1960s, a time when children were raised to obey adults without question. He was an adult, so Rose and her friend felt obliged to obey. Neither of them knew anything about sex, and neither of them told their parents what was happening.

"I didn't know how to handle what had happened to me," Rose says regretfully, "and I became suicidal. I knew suicide was a sin, so to deal with it, I turned to God and was baptized, making my public confession of faith to find strength and hope."

But in the following years, Rose was again molested by the son of a family friend. Again she heard the admonitions: "Rose, if you tell anyone, you'll get into big trouble."

The sins of these men left deep scars on Rose's heart, so

Rose looked for an escape. At first, she found her escape in the pages of science fiction and fantasy novels. She loved the way books transported her out of the world she lived in.

As she grew older, she discovered that the side effect of pain pills legitimately prescribed by her doctor was also a numbing kind of escape. This worked even better than reading. Rose discovered alcohol, and she enjoyed the toxic combination of painkillers and liquor. Adding marijuana was another effective way to numb the pain.

Rose remembers, "All this time I was attending church faithfully with my family, going to youth group and other church activities. I thought my faith was very strong. It wasn't until years later that I realized I was a broken and fractured person living two lives, controlled by my sinful choices." The churchgoing Rose believed in Jesus. The drug-abuser Rose was spiraling downward into a very dark existence.

"The trauma of the rapes caused me to spiral inward even more. Suicide was overwhelming my thought life. It was like God was close by but I could not quite reach out to Him. I was both dead and alive. I was half living my life away from God and half aware He was with me.... He carried me for many years."

Rose got married as soon as she turned eighteen. Steve was a good Christian man, who understood Rose's past and why she didn't want to have any children. She could not handle herself, she told him, let alone the responsibility of a baby. And even if she could, Rose had read that if a person was abused as a child, she would in turn abuse her own children. She didn't want anyone to go through the inward torment she had been through. Steve agreed to no children.

The first time Rose got pregnant, she aborted the baby. But three months later, she was pregnant again. This time Steve stepped in and refused to let her terminate another pregnancy.

Rose was devastated. Not wanting to harm another person, she immediately quit smoking, drinking, and doing drugs. But as the delivery date drew near, she began to panic. She tried to talk Steve into letting her oldest sister and her husband adopt the baby. They desperately wanted children and weren't able to have them. To Rose, it was a win-win situation, but Steve disagreed.

When Sarah was born, Rose would not allow herself to bond with her. She believed she would have to leave before Sarah was old enough to know her, and didn't see a reason to get too close. As Sarah's first birthday quickly passed, the fractured part of Rose started guiding her decisions. She believed it was inevitable that she would abuse her daughter because "they" said it would happen.

Rose's relationship with Steve started to fall apart. He spent long hours at his job and criticized how Rose looked after their baby, which crushed what small bit of self-esteem she had. Devastated, Rose started drinking and using drugs again.

Rose's mother-in-law came to help with baby Sarah. Rose knew it was a matter of time before they all found out she drank and did drugs, and she waited for everyone to disown her.

"I thought my life was ruined at twenty years old. The darkness consumed me."

But unexpectedly, Rose's father, who had never been close to his children, came to her and told her how much he loved her. This shocked Rose—she had no idea anyone loved her that much. In the midst of the darkness, this was the "still, small voice" that gave her the courage to reach out to God.

She left Steve and went first to her parents' house and then to rehab. Looking back now, Rose knows this was the best thing she could have done.

"I wish I could say everything was great after my decision to give up drugs. But it was 'three steps forward and twenty steps back' for many years. I went through more failed relationships and marriages. But even through broken relationships, God showed me He was there for me. The longer I remained sober, the easier it was for me to see God at work in my life."

Rose started to see the thread of grace in her life. She grew up knowing about God's grace and love. She heard the Word of God in her home. Her family loved her through bad choices. No longer did she feel like the fractured Rose was ruling her behavior. She knew she could offer her weaknesses to God and receive His strength in return.

"I'm at a place now where I can talk about my experiences with those going through similar struggles. I can embrace my whole story and honestly say, 'It is well with my soul.' God's grace has covered it all. I love the time I've spent volunteering at a crisis pregnancy center. It's a blessing to use the darkest time in my life to bring hope to others. I can honestly tell them, 'All things work together for good for those that trust God.' I don't feel devastated to the core of my being anymore. God has given me sure footing."

Caitlin
Won Over

Growing up, Caitlin straddled two worlds.

Her first world:

"Another virgin." The satisfied smile of the older boy snaked across his face as he tugged on his jeans. He lived in the neighborhood, and had been touching her for years while she was playing in the nearby fields or swimming in the neighborhood pool.

Thirteen-year-old Caitlin felt nothing but dirty and ashamed. She didn't tell a soul about what happened for the next twenty years.

Caitlin's second world:

Sawdust encircled her slender feet. She sat on a wooden pew, the cathedral a barn overhead. In that atmosphere, surrounded by Jesus' power, Caitlin believed.

Every summer Caitlin visited the Christian camp with her grandmother. Her grandmother's very real faith is one of Caitlin's most vivid childhood memories, and it added to the power of her experience. But after the rape, Caitlin's worlds collided. Her grandmother's love was not enough to convince Caitlin that God could love her after what happened.

To make the pain go away, Caitlin started taking crystal

meth in ninth grade, initiating a nineteen-year addiction that took her on a harrowing, painful journey.

When she was seventeen, Caitlin's brother Jason was in a life-threatening car accident. Caitlin's parents traveled often to be near him in the hospital, and Caitlin fended for herself in their empty home. Without supervision, she started to steal to get money for drugs.

Her parents' marriage didn't survive the stress, and they divorced. When her dad announced he was moving across the country, Caitlin realized she needed a fresh start and went with him. She quit using and met Tim, whose parents were Christians. "I started feeling like a human being," she says. "I wasn't 'the slut' anymore." But even Christians give in to temptation, and Caitlin got pregnant with Tim's baby. He asked her to marry him.

But Caitlin couldn't do it. "I run when I'm scared," she says. So she ran. In the middle of the night, she jumped out of a two-story window and ran to her former drug dealer in another state. She had an abortion and lived in his trailer. Together they did meth. She got pregnant again, then ran again.

After giving birth to her daughter, she met Larry, who was addicted to pain pills and beat her. Caitlin's brother Jason, who had been diagnosed with mental problems as a result of his traumatic head injury, stayed with them. Despite his own problems, he consistently encouraged Caitlin to get her life back together.

Larry and Caitlin had a son, but Larry took too many pills and Caitlin found him, overdosed and dead. In a panic, she ran away again, taking her children but leaving her brother behind.

Caitlin got hooked on meth again, even as tendrils of her former relationship with God reached into her life. She prayed, "Oh God, please let me quit." She read her Bible stoned. She kept using.

Jason visited her, bought her a trailer and painted it. He seemed to be getting better, but not long after he went back home, he killed himself. Jason's suicide haunts Caitlin today. "I know he wouldn't have killed himself if I had stayed with him."

Caitlin was notorious in the small town she lived in—she was known to supply drugs, had *the* party house, and lived a promiscuous, out-of-control life—but the police couldn't get enough evidence to arrest her. Finally, though, squad cars pulled into her driveway and a detective told her, "We're taking the kids." Caitlin watched as the police officer picked up her young son and placed him gently into the back of a patrol car.

"You'd think that a mother who lost her kids would quit, but I couldn't." Instead, she used more and more. As her teeth rotted and her eyes grew hollow, Caitlin looked like a walking dead woman. In desperation, she called her caseworker. "I'm leaving right now to jump off the bridge. Please make sure my father gets my kids." Fueled by what she now calls hope, in the next breath, she said, "But if you come right now, I will go to treatment." Then she hung up.

Terrified of what she'd said, Caitlin rushed through the house, trying to find a hiding place. She cowered in her bathtub, but the caseworker found her. She spent twelve days in detox (most people take seven days or less) while her kids stayed in foster care. After twenty-two days, she was able to visit her children briefly, but she was no better. She swore at her counselors, defiantly challenging everything they said. She kicked and screamed and railed, all the while listening to a voice in her head that told her to just leave. Three months into treatment, her son was allowed to stay with her while her daughter remained in foster care. But Caitlin still resisted treatment.

The staff placed a contract before her that said if she left, she'd lose custody of her children forever. And if she stayed and made another mistake, she'd be kicked out and lose custody. Her only option, if she wanted to keep her children, was to sober up. Caitlin battled in her mind, back and forth, wrestling, wrangling, and losing. "I'm going to leave," she told her caseworker. An evil voice in her head continued to tell her, "You don't need to be here. Leave, get some drugs, and everything will be fine."

Even as the authorities came to take away her son, she begged God to help her. "I started to cry like there was no tomorrow. I yelled at God to please help me, while fifteen women watched me struggle for my kids in the fight of my life.

"I told God, 'You have to help me. I don't have the answers anymore. Please help.' I walked in and signed the contract, but there was an evil force trying very hard to get me to walk out. My hand was shaking. I could hardly make myself sign it. But it was the best day of my whole life."

Something lifted in Caitlin when she signed. Other residents noticed the change and started calling her a Holy Roller. She started prayer groups in the rehab center. "I prayed every minute of every day. I can remember yelling at God, 'You want all this? Take it; it's Yours.' I felt like a stallion that had just been broken. My body ached. I went to every class they offered, and I prayed. I attended my first service at the Salvation Army church. I stumbled to the altar, asking Jesus to help me. I told Him everything I'd done, how much I loved my kids, how I needed His help."

Since then, Caitlin has worked hard at being a good mom, though guilt and shame haunt her. Three years drug-free, she can't think about the day her children were taken away without crying. "Every day, I'm proving to my kids that life will be okay. I have no desire to have meth in my life ever again."

Caitlin sings songs to Jesus, amazed at all He's done. And across the aisle, worshipping in the same church, are the three police officers she used to run from and the caseworker who took away her kids.

The meth user known for drugs, stealing, and promiscuity recently walked into her children's school. At the end-of-the-year assembly, the principal rose. He said, "Our little town is like a village, and there are school volunteers in our village who make a difference. Our children see positive things in our volunteers' lives, making an impact on our students' education. I would like to have the following volunteers come forward to receive special recognition." The principal read off a dozen or so names. Then he smiled and said Caitlin's name. On steady feet, with clear eyes, Caitlin accepted a keychain engraved with "I make a difference."

Naomi
Running toward Love

Sixteen-year-old Naomi didn't know why her pain was so deep. She had a wonderful family, with Christian parents and a house full of brothers and sisters. She lived in a beautiful area of New England, surrounded by horses and rolling hills. And yet for four years, Naomi's dark moods drove her to experiment with alcohol, pills, smoking, cutting, unhealthy emotional relationships, and sex. And when those weren't enough to soothe her troubled soul, she stopped eating.

Naomi started cutting herself and drinking when she was fourteen. Before long, she was sneaking out of the house regularly to meet friends and down rum and Coke, do drugs, hook up, and then drive home drunk. "At that point I didn't care enough about my life to stop," she remembers. "I purposely put myself in dangerous situations."

Her parents went to church regularly, but she hated going. "When I prayed, I screamed at God, 'Why do I feel like this? This is Your fault!'" When people tried to talk to her about what was wrong, she pushed them away, believing she deserved the pain. Naomi didn't have words for what she felt. Instead she dealt with it by inflicting physical abuse on herself.

When her parents went to a weeklong conference and left

her home alone, Naomi found herself standing in front of the medicine cabinet, longing for the release of prescription pills. She took fifteen painkillers, went to her room, and cut herself. She waited for the drugs' numbing qualities to overcome the self-inflicted pain, but instead Naomi started to feel violently dizzy and had trouble breathing. She'd been eating less and had lost a lot of weight, and the pills were too much for her malnourished body to handle.

Naomi panicked and called a friend from school. The friend called Naomi's sister, who was an adult and living on her own. They found Naomi almost passed out, bleeding from her cuts and barely breathing. They called 911.

For two days, Naomi stayed in the hospital, her arms wrapped and her head spinning as the pills cleared out of her system. Overwhelmed, Naomi's parents offered to send her to a residential program two thousand miles away that emphasized physical labor and intense counseling to help troubled girls overcome emotional and physical problems.

Naomi had no more strength to fight for her own life and allowed her parents to take her. But when she got to the program, she held back from the community. She was convinced the hole in her heart could not be healed. She tolerated therapy and did what she was asked, but she felt more isolated than ever. She couldn't understand or explain why she felt and acted the way she did.

Halfway across the country and working through her own issues, Naomi's sister made a shocking announcement. She had pieced together confusing childhood memories and realized that she and Naomi had both been molested when they were small children. Naomi didn't remember what her sister described—she had been too young—but her sister's memories explained why they had both struggled so much with their behavior and emotions.

Reeling from the news, which explained her emotional issues but opened up new channels of anger and resentment, Naomi ran away again. On a weekend when she was supposed to visit her older brother, she made her way instead to a nearby city. For three days, she wandered the streets alone. She hitchhiked and got into cars with strange men. Only by God's grace did no one hurt her.

One of the men who picked her up was kind and concerned, and Naomi found herself sharing her story. The man convinced her to go back to her brother's house. He dropped her off at the bus station, not knowing that, hours earlier, the station had received a poster with Naomi's picture. The ticket agent recognized her and called the police, who took her to a juvenile detention center for two days until her father could travel from the East Coast to get her.

In jail, Naomi finally recognized how dangerous her behavior had become. "I had walked for days, but no matter how far I went, the pain stayed with me." Running obviously wasn't the way to solve her problems. And what she saw in the detention center was frightening. "This was where I would end up if I continued on this path. I didn't want to stay in that place."

Naomi went back to the rehabilitation program with a new attitude. She dove into her therapy, ready to unpack and overcome her sexual abuse and self-destructive behavior. Despite many ups and downs, she felt she was making real progress toward healing, and so did her therapist.

But over several months, the directors and staff noticed a new problem with Naomi. Even as she opened her heart to talk about her experiences, she shut down other behaviors, like eating. Despite the long hours of physical activity required of all residents, Naomi trimmed back her portions at meals to unhealthy levels.

Naomi, at four feet eleven, weighed only eighty pounds when her father refused to let her come home for a visit, concerned that the family could not care for her in her condition. It seemed that even her program counselors might be ready to give up. In a last-ditch effort, the program's motherly director confronted her.

"This is your choice between life and death," she told the shrunken, emaciated girl. "We want to help you, but we can't do the work for you. You have to choose it."

It was the message Naomi needed to hear. Empowered, she did make the choice—to eat, first of all, but also to walk away from her past. She accepted at last that she could not control or dwell in her own pain, and started to accept the truth that the program staff had shown her all along—that she was loved and that she was worthy of love.

Naomi started praying again during those months. "I was around people who loved God and shared it every day, and it had an impact on me.... The way they talked about God meant something to me."

Under the patient care of the staff, Naomi's body and heart healed, and after two years, she completed an emotional graduation ceremony and committed to take the second chance she had been given to live. "I know the pain will never fully go away, but I have been taught how to live despite the pain."

She is home now, finishing her high school studies and looking forward to college. And instead of running away from the pain, she has learned to run to God in her pain. "Life gets tough sometimes, but I know that, because of what I've been through, I am stronger for it. I wouldn't trade my experiences for another life, because I know God has a purpose in all this and He will make everything beautiful in its time."

Jill

A God-Shaped Emptiness

*J*ill spent ten years frantically trying to fill the spiritual void in her life.

Her family moved a lot while she was growing up, and Jill had six different homes before sixth grade. Her father was a pastor, but she never learned how to pursue a relationship with Jesus. "Church was a façade," she says. "I tuned out during my dad's sermons, attacked the refreshments after the service, and split as soon as the cookies ran out."

Jill concentrated instead on what she could see in the mirror. Tall and thin, she was graced with a model's figure. High school became part fashion show and part dating game. Boys consumed her mental energy, and she sacrificed her sexual purity, one step at a time, to win affirmation. At sixteen, after months of resisting sex yet experimenting in other ways, she couldn't defend her reasons for abstinence and surrendered to her boyfriend's coaxing.

Sex opened a new hole in Jill's heart, and she sped up the pace of her life while she tried to fill it. She lied to her parents and her friends about where she was, fabricating activities to bury the truth of her escapades. "I knew I was rejecting God through these lies, but the greatest lies I told were to myself:

that sexual relationships could meet my needs, that they were perfectly acceptable before marriage, and that I didn't really need friends or a church."

Sex was only one part of her increasingly frenetic lifestyle. Jill tried to stay away from home as much as possible. She worked after school at a trendy boutique that paid for her growing wardrobe. She'd do her homework at the shop, rush to the gym for a long workout, and suck down a diet shake for dinner on her way to her boyfriend's house, where she would stay until it was time to drive home after everyone else was asleep.

Before the end of high school, Jill started to model occasionally; she loved the validation. After she graduated, she decided to pursue fashion full-time.

Without structure, Jill's life sank into a dangerous series of addictions. The modeling industry, with its emphasis on physical perfection, sucked Jill into a spiral of self-loathing and uncertainty. Food began to control her, as did her pursuit of the perfect body and a steady stream of boyfriends.

"Men became objects to me, things I chewed through to boost my barrel-scraping self-esteem. I'd flirt, kiss, have sex, ignore, manipulate, blame, and discard as carelessly as I'd binge on a bag of Oreos. Either way, in the morning I'd always wake up with the slimy taste of shame in my mouth. I'd force myself into two or three hours at the gym to burn off the thousands of calories I'd consumed. When I had to work at the boutique, I'd adorn my prized body with expensive outfits that I sold to myself at a dishonest discount."

The madness continued for two years, until promiscuity, over-exercise, laxative abuse, and shopping addiction gave way to physical pain. Bunions on Jill's feet worsened as she ran faster and faster from God. Pain made working difficult, and money became tight.

But Jill wasn't ready to give up her race for perfection. Instead, she invested thousands of dollars she didn't have in a personal trainer, who got her into shape for a modeling contract in Europe. She thought moving overseas would be the bandage she needed to patch up her crumbling life. Instead, she spent months in a country where she knew no one and didn't speak the language. Lonely and confused, Jill went back to her old addictions. She kept the translations for *laxative* in her wallet for her frequent efforts to undo the damage of binges. She met traveling American men and slept with them. She started smoking cigarettes. Her pain drew her to attend an international church a few times, but she returned home just as battered and emotionally bruised as when she had left.

Life seemed hopeless. Modeling jobs trickled in, but her feet were so badly damaged that she could hardly work. She describes that time as a period of "purposelessness. I'd shut myself in my room with wine and a movie. I'd smoke cigarettes all day long. I worked out, and that was my life. I'd walk to the gym and back (four miles total) and work out for hours. Smoking, drinking, binging, spending. I was in a time warp, going nowhere, being nobody. I was completely empty."

God had her right where He wanted her.

After a few months, Jill moved for a modeling job and met William—tall, blond, blue-eyed, and Christian. "God knew to reach me through one of my addictions: handsome men," she says. "William wouldn't sleep with me, but he prayed with me, asked about my heart, or about my journey, or about my thoughts on God. Never before had I been challenged or pursued in this way! It felt so real, so meaningful. I was laughing again! Learning to love, to feel." They dated long-distance from that day forward, talking on the phone every day.

While William was showing Jill what a healthy relationship

looked like, God was using Jill's exercise addiction as well. One day she prayed for Him to give her a friend, and the next day she ran into a former modeling acquaintance at the gym. The two immediately struck up a conversation—something that had always been hard for Jill to do with women—and made plans to get together. Several weeks later, her new friend invited her to church, and Jill found a community that could sustain her.

With William's support and the encouragement of her new church, Jill's heart softened enough for God to bring a final catalyst. The bunions that had plagued Jill for years required surgery, and recovery left her unable to get around for almost three months. "I was stuck again, but this time it felt safe. I could hear God say, 'Jill, I am giving you new feet. Are you going to follow Me with them?'" With nowhere to run, Jill finally felt the warmth of a loving God, and surrendered herself to Him.

Today, she is in a program for her eating disorder and therapy for her issues with men. Unexpectedly, God called her to break up with William, and Jill obeyed, ready to commit to depending solely on God for a season, without the distractions of male attention that had controlled her behavior for so long.

Jill tells her story whenever she has the chance, believing God uses every dirty secret she kept for His glory. When she tells people about the way she used to live, they do not believe her. They cannot imagine that she used to tramp around in secret, dirtying sheets, stealing, lying, cheating, and abusing.

"God has worked a miracle. I see now that, with every choice I make to trust Him, whether in surrendering the need to buy a shirt or pursue a man, I'm giving Him room to do things more amazing than I could imagine. That hunger inside of me is a good thing, a God-created thing that only He can fill and is willing to fill."

Jenn
Escaping the Grief

Jenn got out of the car carefully, trying not to catch her pink prom dress on her silver heels. "Do you think Mom is throwing us an after-prom party?" Jenn asked her date when she noticed all the cars and people.

Before she could find out, her date's dad was there in front of them. "Jenn, I'm afraid something terrible has happened."

She saw the worry on his face. Their families had been friends so long, she knew him as well as she knew her own father.

Her father. Something must have happened. Earlier that day her grandfather had died of a heart attack. Her father had flown to Wisconsin to help with funeral preparations. Dad was twenty years older than her mother. *Did he have a heart attack, too?*

"What's going on?" Jenn asked, not sure she wanted to know the answer.

"It's Eric. He's . . . he's dead."

Eric. Her fourteen-year-old brother. *What kind of crazy joke is this? Fourteen-year-olds don't die.* But she heard the sounds of grief coming from the house. It was real.

Eric had been hanging out with a couple of friends when another boy from a few neighborhoods over showed up. They all went to the same school, and for years, the other boy had made fun of Eric's weight.

According to witnesses, Eric decided to speak up. A fight ensued, and the other boy pulled out a knife and stabbed Eric in the heart. His best friend, his ten-year-old brother, and his brother's friend watched helplessly.

Eric died instantly.

"They arrested the killer and took statements from the witnesses. The detectives just left," Jenn's family told her.

Like the rhinestones that lined her pink dress, her tears sparkled as they slowly dripped off her cheeks. Jenn's lips quivered as she spoke. "Why didn't someone call me?"

"There was nothing you could do."

Not even say good-bye.

The shock was followed by a paralyzing numbness. "Before my brother died, my goal was to graduate from high school, go to college, become a lawyer, and get married," says Jenn. "All of a sudden, nothing was certain. I didn't have plans anymore; I didn't have goals. I didn't have anything to look forward to."

Eleven long months passed before the trial began. Though he was only fourteen, the boy who killed Eric was charged with first-degree murder. The trial lasted three days and included emotional testimonies from the young witnesses. The defense claimed it was self-defense, but Jenn didn't see it that way at all.

The jury did, though. Deliberations were short, and the verdict was clear: *not guilty*.

"It was one month before the anniversary of his death, and it was like it happened all over again," remembers Jenn.

Jenn's mom had raised her kids to believe in God. They had gone to church every Sunday for a while. Even when they later stopped going, Jenn heard about God from the sermons her mom listened to and watched on TV and the Christian music she listened to. After Eric died, these things helped her mother cope. But Jenn decided she no longer believed in God.

"I was so mad at even the *thought* of God, it completely turned me off," says Jenn.

Jenn's mom turned to God for comfort. Jenn turned to drugs.

"I smoked pot for the first time after my brother died." But the marijuana wasn't strong enough to soothe her emotions. Repressed anger became clinical depression. Then panic attacks. She visited a psychiatrist who prescribed a heavy dose of Xanax. "The drugs totally made me not feel anything. If I was sad, if I was nervous, if I was angry, whatever it was, if I took one of those, I didn't feel anything."

That became her goal—to not feel anything. To be numb.

"I started hanging around people who could get drugs for me. My crowd of friends completely changed. I started getting into trouble." Jenn spent a year on probation for getting caught with pot in her car. Her license was taken away. But she continued to use.

She started dating her supplier—he was cute and always ready for a good time. They hung out and partied together. A year and a half later, she was pregnant. "At that point I had to slow down, but I couldn't stop," says Jenn. Despite her drug use, her son was born healthy.

Jenn continued using prescription painkillers, taking Xanax, and smoking pot after her son's birth. "I tried to wean myself off but I couldn't. I panicked if I thought about not taking the pills."

A few months after giving birth, Jenn got pregnant again. This time, she married her boyfriend, but she continued her drug use. It was a miracle when her daughter was also born healthy. Jenn responded by taking even more drugs. "They were something I had to have. If I couldn't have them, I was sick. I couldn't do anything without them."

The drug use she'd once tried to control was now officially out of control. "I was this person I didn't even know anymore. I had a part-time job as a waitress, but all my money was spent on pills. I'd go to the doctor. I'd have other people get them for me. My whole focus was on getting drugs. Our family worried and didn't know what to do, but they didn't know how bad it was, because I hid it from them. I was always functioning," says Jenn, who was now taking up to twenty different kinds of drugs: painkillers, Xanax, and muscle relaxants. Occasionally, she drank alcohol as well.

But the drugs caught up with her. Jenn was arrested for driving under the influence. Her family no longer trusted her. Even her husband, who used drugs himself from time to time, couldn't understand why she was hooked—he could stop whenever he felt like it.

During a particularly vicious fight with her mother, Jenn said horrible things she soon regretted. When she called to ask for forgiveness, she broke down. Jenn didn't see any hope for escaping the life she'd created. "Mom, I need some help," Jenn cried.

Her family arranged for Jenn to enter a Christian treatment center. It required a yearlong residential commitment. "My family said, 'We can't make you stay, but if you don't, we're not going to let you see your kids. You won't have a place to live. We'll call the authorities, whatever we have to do, but you won't have contact with any of us.'"

Jenn knew she'd hit bottom. With no other options, she agreed to the treatment.

At first, she thought the religious stuff they talked about was "crap." But over time, she gave it a try. "I wasn't dumb enough to think *I'm right, and all these people are wrong*," says Jenn. "Little by little, God just melted my heart. He softened it. My eyes were opened. It was as if I had been living in this cloud of smoke, not seeing what was in front of me. Then things started to make sense. Like the Bible—I can totally see how it relates to today. It's not just an old book. It's now; it's forever. God's amazing. Every day my eyes are opened to new things."

In rehab, Jenn found hope. "The board members took us out to eat once a month. I couldn't believe so many people cared. I had no idea there were people like that in the world. They taught me about a God who was loving and forgiving. And it wasn't just them trying to *tell* me. I was *shown*. I was shown by the dedication of the volunteers, by their care, and by the love that everybody had for me. They loved us and would do anything for us."

Jenn graduated from the program and returned to her family drug-free. For the first time since Eric died, she wanted to feel—to feel the joy and love she'd found in Jesus.

Her turnaround changed her whole family. Her husband got a job and got clean. Together they're raising their children to love the God she once didn't care to know. Now Jenn has dreams and plans for her future. She looks forward to eternity in heaven, where one day she'll introduce her son to his uncle—a high worth waiting for.

part three

Family
Problems

In the beginning…

Leah

eah was not a pretty girl, and everyone knew it—
including Leah.

It was said that she had "weak eyes." In her day, that may
have meant she was nearsighted, cross-eyed, sensitive to light,
or that she had syphilis of the eyes, which would have left them
red, infected, and oozing. Whatever the case, this wasn't a
pretty girl.

But her sister, Rachel, was described as "lovely in form, and
beautiful" (Genesis 29:17, NIV). In other words, Rachel was
drop-dead gorgeous *and* had a great body. Even their father,
Laban, when he named them, appeared to prefer Rachel (which
meant "lamb" or "ewe") over his firstborn daughter, Leah
("wild cow").[1]

Each girl had a job. Leah cooked and cleaned house. Rachel
worked as a shepherdess. The physical work agreed with
Rachel's developing body. She was tan and fit. She worked
alongside other shepherds. Everyone knew her and loved her.
Rachel had everything a man could want in a wife. Leah?

Well, she could cook.

And she was the oldest. Birth order was an important religious and cultural consideration. At that time, a firstborn
enjoyed certain rights and privileges. One of those was that
she'd be the first to marry, and in their community, girls married early—while they were still teenagers.

Leah was probably home preparing the evening meal when she first heard the news: her father had invited a foreigner to stay with them. Hoping this was the suitor she'd been looking for, Leah washed up, combed her hair, and put on a veil so he wouldn't notice her weak eyes. Perhaps he'd be more open-minded than the local men, who laughed at wild-cow jokes and made fun of her appearance.

The foreigner's name was Jacob. He was handsome and strong. More important, he was a distant relative. (It was a desirable thing to keep it all in the family.) Seeing him, Leah felt a warm tingling in her stomach. She hoped her cooking would be enough to impress him, and she hurried to get the food on the table. One bite of an unleavened biscuit and Jacob would be all hers. After all, as the oldest daughter, she was to be the first to marry. She had to be thanking God for her good fortune as she finished dinner preparations.

Somewhere between the main course and dessert, Jacob told them what had happened at the well. He had stopped to water his animals and was waiting for more shepherds to arrive so that together they could move the huge rock that covered the mouth of the well.

"I was asking if anyone knew your family," said Jacob, "and then Rachel appeared. She was so beautiful, I moved the rock by myself!"

"He did," said Rachel, giggling like a school girl. "All by himself!"

Laban frowned.

Rachel blushed.

At that moment, Leah knew that Jacob, just like every other man she'd ever met, felt something—not for her, but for Rachel. She also knew from the blushing and giggling that Rachel felt something, too.

Over the next few weeks, Jacob worked for the family. Leah tried to catch his attention with food, friendly conversation, and acts of service. Kind, but never interested, Jacob focused all his attention on the lovely Rachel.

Leah's worst fears were confirmed when Laban asked Jacob to set a price for his labor. Jacob, completely smitten with Rachel, said, "I'll work for seven years if you'll let me marry Rachel."

"Better you than some other guy," said Laban, and they shook hands.

Leah was crushed. Not only did the love of her life choose her *sister*, but her father went against every cultural and religious norm they believed to let his second daughter get betrothed before his first. It was enough to make a good girl lose her religion.

After seven years of working the land, and not one day more, Jacob didn't even try to hide his excitement. "Give me my wife. I want to lie with her."

It had been seven years. Leah still didn't have a suitor. Now she'd watch the one she loved marry her sister.

Laban invited friends, neighbors, and family to a feast prepared by Leah. At the end of the celebration, Laban brought Jacob his bride. By now, everyone was a little tipsy. It was late, it was dark, and the bride was veiled from head to sandal.

Unbeknownst to Jacob, Laban had switched daughters. Jacob retired to his room with his new wife, thinking it was the beautiful Rachel, but in fact, it was Leah.

Did Leah think it was a good idea to trick Jacob? And her sister? Or was she so desperate, she didn't think she had another choice? *I'm so ugly, who else would want me?* Perhaps she thought a night alone with Jacob would convince him of her charms. Whatever her thoughts, imagine her pain.

It was dark when she unveiled herself and Jacob lay with her. Perhaps he stroked her hair and said things like, "Rachel, I've waited so long for this moment," or "You're so beautiful, Rachel." Was this the first and last time Leah heard words like these? Did she close her eyes and just for a moment think he was actually talking to her instead of her sister?

She must have feared the sunrise. What would Jacob do when he found out she'd agreed to the date-and-switch plan?

The next morning, Jacob was spitting mad. As she pulled the blanket around her, Leah heard him yelling at Laban from the next room. "You cheated me. You're a liar and a deceiver."

Cunning Laban worked out a deal. If Jacob agreed to work for seven more years, he would also give him Rachel. But first, Jacob must finish out his honeymoon week with Leah.

That week, Leah must have tried everything to make him love her. But as is so often the case, the harder she tried, the less desirable she became. Her plan failed. At the end of the week, Jacob still loved Rachel more than Leah.

We don't know what happened to Leah's faith over the next few years, but there are clues. Leah got pregnant and gave birth to a son. She named him Reuben, saying, "The Lord has noticed my misery and now my husband will love me." Almost identical statements were made at the birth of kids two and three, Simeon and Levi. Leah's entire focus was on having children to make her husband love her.

But something happened to change all that. Did she learn that, no matter what she did, she couldn't make Jacob love her? Did she finally come to the conclusion that she couldn't control her husband—only her own actions? Or perhaps she experienced God in a way that made Him more personal to her.

By the time she had her fourth child, Judah, Leah didn't even mention Jacob. Instead she said, "Now I will praise the Lord."

What caused her turnaround? We don't know. We just know that she had one. For the first time since meeting Jacob, Leah appeared to be focused on God, thanking Him for the blessings in her life. And this new attitude continued with her fifth and sixth sons, whom she believed were blessings from God.

By the time her daughter was born, Leah trusted God completely. Her baby was named Dinah, meaning "God is in control."

Truly He is. There was never evidence Jacob loved Leah as he loved Rachel. Yet Leah loved Jacob until she died. Despite her obstacles, she spent the majority of her years drawing closer to God, pouring out her grief to Him, relying on Him to supply her needs, and trusting that He was in control.

And ultimately God's covenant with Abraham flowed through Leah, not Rachel. The lineage of Jesus is through Leah's son Judah's tribe. The same son who was the turning point of her faith became the ancestor to the turning point of our faith—Jesus.

Not only did God reward her faithfulness, but so did Jacob. Rachel's body was buried in the desert, yet Leah's body lies in the family tomb next to her husband.

Abraham Kuyper once wrote, "There are two kinds of beauty. There is the beauty which God gives at birth, and which withers as a flower. And there is the beauty which God grants when, by His grace, men are born again. That kind of beauty never vanishes but blooms eternally."[2]

Rachel may have gotten her beauty at birth, but Leah's blooms eternally.

Liz

A Princess Pursued

Liz grew up in a house full of hatred and anger. Her older brother was angry and mean to her. Her father was angry and mean to her brother. Over time, she came to believe that anger and rejection were reality.

As a small child, Liz prayed to accept Jesus into her heart. "I thought I was Jesus' little princess," she remembers wistfully. She knew without a doubt that Jesus loved her.

But the growing tension in Liz's home made it hard to hold on to those positive beliefs. Liz's adopted brother lashed out at everyone in the family, especially Liz, whom he resented as her parents' "natural" child. Her father turned against him and openly favored Liz, which made her brother act out even more. When the battles raged at home, no one protected her. And slowly, over time, angry words sank in and affected the way Liz saw herself. She felt like her parents rejected her by not protecting her from her brother, and that influenced the way Liz thought about God. "I believed God was rejecting me, that I deserved to be alone and unprotected, that to express my own feelings or needs was selfish. All that talk about love and hope and happiness was a fairy tale; hostility was how people really lived."

Lonely and depressed, Liz sought acceptance elsewhere. She started drinking at parties during her freshman year in high school, and filled her weekends with alcohol and the shallow company of friends who had no idea what real care and loyalty meant. She found comfort with classmates who planned their lives around keg parties and sneaking off to clubs with live music and lenient bouncers who did not check IDs.

Things got worse when Liz was a sophomore. Her home life was chaotic. Her father moved out of the house, telling her that part of the reason he was leaving was that she and her brother couldn't get along. Liz knew she'd disappointed her father. She wasn't thin enough. She wasn't disciplined enough. She was miserable all the time. Her very presence made her brother angry. Liz sank deeper into a numb fog she would later recognize as depression, fed by her father's rejection and her brother's open hostility.

Liz channeled her anger over her family situation toward God. She absorbed her father's skepticism about religion and struggled with the thought that a loving God would allow so much pain in the world, and in her own life. She didn't understand why even scholars disagreed about what the Bible said and meant. Could something so confusing really be true? She decided it wasn't. If God had no power over these things, He must not exist.

One weekend when she was sixteen, Liz was getting ready to go meet her friends. She felt God leaning on her heart, telling her not to drink. Defiantly, Liz answered, "That's just too bad. I'm going to go out and do it anyway."

During her junior year, doctors diagnosed Liz's dad with terminal illness. Knowing he had only a short time left to live, he threw the divorce papers away and moved back to the family home. While he tried to make amends for the disarray he'd created, he never asked for Liz's forgiveness. She struggled through school as her father lost weight and shrank into his illness. He died the day after her graduation.

Liz spent that summer drinking and watching television. "I remember hearing about how kids in gangs were hard to reform because they saw no future for themselves. They didn't mind dying at twenty-two because they didn't see what good could happen after that, anyhow. I totally agreed with that."

Liz's grades had never been good. She spent more time with her friends than paying attention in class, and the tempers flaring at home further distracted her. But in her family, each child was expected to attend a residential four-year college. She applied to only a few schools, and only two accepted her. One required girls to wear a skirt every day. She wasn't sure she could do that, so she went to the other school, a Christian college near her home.

She wasn't excited about going to a Christian school, but she thought she could handle it. She was comfortable around Christians, despite how she felt about God. Liz expected college to be like the youth group she attended occasionally in high school—more social than spiritual.

What she found instead changed her life. Within a week, she knew the college was another world. She experienced real worship for the first time in a chapel service. The students around her loved God with passion and fully believed He loved them in return. Her professors were smart, educated people who could answer every intellectual challenge she threw at them. But more important, none of the Christians she met ridiculed her. No one made her feel small or less valuable than everyone around her. They embraced her for who she was—numb, overweight, sarcastic, and all. For the first time, Liz felt seen.

She moved from darkness to light quickly, but her emotional healing took time. At school, Liz found a safe place to grieve her father's death and deal with her anger at him. By her sophomore year, she was ready to tackle the subject of God, and the difference between the distant, judgmental Creator she thought she knew and the personal, passionate Father her friends and professors talked about. That year, she took a course that explained how God, from the beginning of time, orchestrated history by raising up the people who would produce a Messiah, who was God and who would sacrifice His life. He accomplished this and poured out His Spirit into everyone who had faith, and it was the job of Christians to respond to His love by proclaiming this to all the corners of the earth. He did have a plan. And He had called Liz to be part of His healing and grace! Her life had a purpose; there was something and Someone to live for.

Accepting God's love changed Liz's life. Instead of going back home after graduation to drink her life away, Liz went to work in the inner city and became a teacher. She moved overseas, full of the confidence that comes with God's love, and served as a missionary to poor families there for three years. Today she's studying for the next step in her journey. "God sees me and loves me," she says with confidence. "God has not only forgiven me; He has pursued me and brought powerful healing through the Word, loving friends, transformation in my family, and a wonderful sense of purpose."

Bridget
Welcoming Home the Homeless

ridget's parents divorced before she turned two. Her mother remarried, and Bridget grew up bouncing around the country with her mother, stepfather, and several stepsiblings. She did not thrive in the tumultuous environment, and by the time Bridget was in junior high, she was sneaking out of the house to go to parties. Her parents put her in a number of schools to try to help her. Finally, they enrolled her in a private Christian high school.

There she met Debbie. Debbie's family was going skiing, so she couldn't use her ticket to a revival. "You can go in my place," she said, and handed Bridget the ticket. "Oh, and can you give me your address? I'll send you a postcard."

Bridget's experience at the revival changed her heart. "I had my first real encounter with the Spirit of God at that revival," she says. And Debbie kept her word, sending Bridget a postcard.

During chapel at school, Debbie asked, "Bridget, have you been saved?"

"No. I don't know what that is."

Debbie talked about Jesus' ability to save someone from her sins, then asked, "Do you want to be saved?"

Bridget nodded and walked down the aisle at the chapel service. She looked behind her, surprised to see Debbie coming with her. Debbie held Bridget's hand and prayed with her.

From that moment, Debbie and Bridget were best friends. Bridget started getting better grades and making wise choices, but her family's problems kept pulling her down. Her stepdad invited a friend to come live with them, even though relationships in Bridget's house were always tense. Her mom and stepdad spent more and more time screaming at each other during escalating fights.

So it wasn't a huge surprise when Bridget's mom picked her and her sister up from school in a U-Haul. Her stepdad's friend was at the wheel—apparently he was Mom's new boyfriend. They drove away, not letting Bridget say good-bye to her stepfather or to Debbie, and headed across the country.

Bridget's mom eventually kicked her boyfriend out and invited Bridget's stepdad to move in with them again to work things out. But things were not smooth. One day Bridget's mom pulled her daughter aside. "Honey," she said, "I don't want you telling anyone, but I'm trying to locate an ex-boyfriend. He's in prison for murder."

She eventually found him, and they started writing letters. She told Bridget, "It's up to you to get the mail every single day. I don't want your stepdad finding out." It didn't make sense to Bridget—after all, her stepfather had endured her mother's unfaithfulness before and raised three kids who weren't his— but she did what her mother asked and hid the imprisoned man's letters in a shoe box in her closet.

One day she forgot to check the mail. Her mom trashed her room, throwing things. "If your stepdad finds out what's going on, I'm taking the other kids and leaving you with him. And you know what? He won't want you, and you'll be homeless."

Bridget, scared, decided to tell him what was going on.

"I'll never let you be homeless," he said. "But I'm going to have to confront your mom when she gets home."

Panicked, Bridget threw her clothes out the window, hoisted herself out, and left home, bumming places to stay over the next two weeks. When her parents found her, they packed the family and moved everyone back to the town where Debbie lived.

By that time, Bridget had again acquired a taste for partying, so when she returned to the same high school Debbie attended, she started to lead two lives—one with Debbie, the other with her partying friends. She got kicked out of her new high school for marijuana use, went to an alternative school, and eventually landed back at the Christian school she used to attend. Debbie's family took Bridget to church and sheltered her in the embrace of a normal, Christian family. They loved her like their own.

But their love was not enough to keep things at home from strangling Bridget. Her mother continued to communicate with her ex-boyfriend in prison. And even though her parents promised her a new car if she kept up her grades, that car soon became a painful reminder of her family's chaos. Yes, they gave her a new car for her birthday as promised, but two months later, her mom announced she was moving back to be near the ex-boyfriend. She asked if Bridget would like to come along, but Bridget said no. Unfazed, her mother packed her own belongings in Bridget's new car and drove away without her daughter, never even saying good-bye.

Distraught, Bridget moved in with a boyfriend. She used ecstasy and partied, slowly cutting herself off from Debbie's family.

Bridget kept in touch with Debbie, but they drifted apart. Still, Debbie reached out to her. One night, Debbie invited Bridget to go with her to a high school football game and said she'd call Bridget to tell her where to meet.

But Friday, then Saturday came without a call. Bridget knew she'd find Debbie at church on Sunday morning, so she went, but Debbie wasn't there.

It wasn't until Monday after school that her boyfriend told her the news. "Your friend Debbie's been in an accident," he told her. Debbie was in the hospital on life support. She'd been in a car accident before the game Friday night and hit her head. The doctors gave her only a fifty percent chance of surviving.

Bridget sped to the hospital. There, in intensive care, lay a comatose Debbie, head shaved, a trickle of blood coming out of her ear. Bridget couldn't talk to her, touch her, apologize. Three days later, Debbie died.

At sixteen, Bridget's life spun wildly out of control. She and her boyfriend fought constantly. Police arrested her on drug-related charges. She dropped out of school. For months, she heard nothing from her family. She became addicted to meth, marijuana, and alcohol. Occasionally, she'd weep her way into church, but nothing seemed to help. She hopped from house to house.

With Debbie's memory always in her mind, Bridget started slowly changing her life. She broke up with her boyfriend when he got arrested, and committed to living a cleaner life. She found an apartment, landed two jobs, and attended church regularly. Even so, the journey's been rough.

"Throughout the years, I have always fallen off, then gotten back on, then fallen off, then repeated it again." Now in her twenties, Bridget is raising her young daughter, owns a home, and attends school. She's been drug-free for three years and plans to take part in a medical mission trip. "My relationship with the Lord is stronger than ever," she says. "I'm just now starting to share my story and be comfortable doing it. It took a lot of persistence. I fell so many times and went back and forth from God to the streets, but here I am today with a story to tell. One that only God could've created to be so wonderful."

In the midst of her transformation, Bridget picked up a pen, finding solace in writing about her journey. She writes, "I am that girl—the one screaming and cussing, the one fighting and slandering, the drunkest girl in the club, the one sitting in jail, the one selling drugs, the one doing drugs, the one lying and cheating, the one who is deceitful, the gossiper, the hypocrite, the alcoholic, the sex addict, the one with no patience. You name it, I've been it. That is me. That is the girl the Lord chose to give mercy and forgiveness to, the one the Lord chose to be weak and lead the strong, the one He blessed with sobriety and a beautiful daughter, the one He guides with unconditional love. I am the prodigal daughter whom He welcomed back home with wide-open arms and clothed in the best clothes and gave food to eat and something to drink. I am that girl."

Dawn
Grace Overflowing

*I*f you were to talk to Dawn, she would say with conviction, "As I look back on my life, I am overwhelmed to
see God's amazing grace that covered me through my most
painful years. His mercy was there all along. I know I don't
deserve this love that God freely gives, but my life is a story of
grace."

Dawn grew up going to church, but she doesn't say she had
a Christian home. Her family had good morals, but she felt the
bondage of legalism as a very young girl. She didn't know about
a personal relationship with Jesus until she was in high school.
When she went to church camp her freshman year, she began to
see God differently. One speaker in particular presented God as
loving and relational. He talked about unconditional love and
Dawn knew he was talking about the real God. For the first
time, she was struck with the idea that it didn't matter how much
she had messed up. The speaker had a peace about him that
Dawn wanted, too. She wanted to know what it felt like to be
loved no matter what. When he read Scripture to the group, she
felt overwhelmed, hearing of how much God loved her. And she
knew it was true. That night, Dawn made a decision to commit
her life to God and jumped into God's love without hesitation,

wanting to wipe away the impersonal, rule-book God she had known.

Dawn knew she couldn't go back to living under the oppression of legalism. "I wanted to erase the image of God I had come to know. I knew Him as a punitive judge. I didn't know 'God is love.' He had been a lawmaker in my life, but not really love."

Dawn joined an area-wide youth group and began connecting with friends who offered support outside the walls of her church. But the enemy was there, too, looking for a weak spot.

Satan came after Dawn, reminding her of everything she had done that was sinful. "I felt there was pressure coming at me that I had not experienced before. He wanted to remind me of God as law, not love."

Dawn was well respected as a leader, and she enjoyed the popularity. Even as her spiritual battle raged, she learned what the people around her expected of her, and she met their expectations. "My friends at school expected me to be the life of the party, and I was well liked and popular. My church friends expected me to be obedient to God, to be respectful, and to have it all together. Whichever group I was in, I'd be whoever they wanted me to be."

But soon enough, it caught up with Dawn and she couldn't keep up the appearance that she had it all together. Boys were her weakness. She lost her virginity at fourteen, and at sixteen she found herself pregnant.

Abortion was never an option. When Dawn told the father of the baby, he offered to marry her, even though they were both so young.

"No. We're putting our baby up for adoption. That's what's best."

Dawn chose to go before her church congregation and ask for forgiveness. She knew what it could mean. The church was very legalistic, and she might be "disfellowshipped" (kicked out). Dawn knew a couple who had been asked to leave because of their divorce. With regret and guilt, Dawn wrote a letter to her church, and one Sunday morning, she went forward and stood before the congregation. "I am sorry . . . but I'm pregnant and I don't want to be a stumbling block to anyone. If you need to ask me to leave, I will."

The minister prayed and dismissed the congregation. As she stood up to leave, Dawn turned around and found the whole church standing behind her. Extended family and friends lined up to embrace her. She never expected this. It was like the love she had felt at camp. Though grace wasn't a concept taught in her little church, this was Dawn's first experience with grace that was so much stronger than her sin.

Over the next few months Dawn struggled with the approaching loss of giving up her baby. She knew she was having a girl, and she wanted little Angela to grow up knowing about grace early in life. But how could she ensure that? The initial plan was for the baby to be adopted by her aunt and uncle, who lived just two houses down. But before Angela was born, they got a call from the agency and chose to adopt a different baby from a young mother they didn't know. God's plan of grace was better. He knew it would have been too difficult for Dawn to see her baby every day. Instead, He brought her to a Christian couple who also wanted a baby. Dawn gave birth to her daughter and spent four precious days with her in the hospital before the adoption agency took her to her new family, and Dawn, still a child herself in many ways, went home to her own.

Through all the drama and heartbreak, Dawn's mother never condemned her for what she had done. She stood firmly beside her daughter, and often told Dawn how much she admired her strength to do the right thing. Then, just as Dawn came home to rebuild her life after Angela's birth, her mother's battle with ovarian cancer took a turn for the worse. She struggled painfully for almost a year, but passed away almost a year after Angela was born.

"My mother told me before she died, 'Dawn, I don't feel worthy to be your mother.' I couldn't believe she felt that way, and it was another outpouring of grace God gave to me before she passed. The emotional pain [of that year] was paralyzing at times." Unable to deal with the grief, Dawn's dad took a job out of state and moved away only a few weeks after his wife's death. Dawn and her brother were left to take care of themselves and run the household. This was not what she thought her senior year in high school was supposed to be like.

Her dad remarried eleven months after her mother's death. Without him around, Dawn found herself always needing a boyfriend, and she continued to be sexually active. College brought her new freedom, which she took advantage of. She drank heavily to relieve her emotional pain, and she kept up her active sexual life. After months of the chaotic lifestyle, Dawn crashed emotionally and began to contemplate suicide. She grieved over her sin. She knew God was so disappointed, but she didn't know how to reach out for His grace again.

Dawn finally reached out to an aunt, one of the only family members she stayed in touch with, and drove all night to get to her home. When she arrived, she poured out her heart before going to sleep, telling the loving older woman everything. "I don't remember everything I confessed to her, but I clearly remember the grace my aunt showered on me."

They talked for a long time, and Dawn began to reach out to the grace of God that was present in the room. Miraculously she recognized who she was at the core: God's child.

Dawn needed a clean start, so she moved to a new city. She

found a job as a bank teller and began going to church regularly. She found entire communities of Christians who showed her the same grace her aunt had, and her mother before that. She grew closer to God and stronger in faith. The cycles of sin that had entangled her throughout her teen years were finally loosened. Today, she is in contact with Angela, who has grown up to be a strong young Christian woman, and she speaks regularly to women and teen groups about relationships.

"God keeps using my pain, my mess, my junk for His purposes. I certainly don't deserve it—His grace still keeps overflowing all around!"

Leslie
A Rich Inheritance

*L*eslie remembers sitting in Sunday school and asking Jesus into her heart when she was about seven years old. As a young girl, she knew He was real, but life was not simple. Leslie's parents got divorced when she was eleven, and her mom remarried quickly. It wasn't an easy transition.

At sixteen, life was getting way too complicated. Leslie was struggling with the effects of divorce, which took a toll on her faith and trust in God.

"I'd squirm and cry through services," she remembers now. "God was speaking to me. I knew I had not really made Him Lord of my life. I was starting to drink to cope with my shattered childhood, but God was calling me to go deeper with Him. I knew I was saved, but I decided to be baptized. Once I committed to this, I felt a huge weight had been lifted, like I knew God and I were really going to start walking together."

God chased Leslie at that time because He knew she needed a deeper relationship with Him in order to handle what would come next. A few months after the baptism, her mom sat down with Leslie and her sister, Donna, and told them that the reason she'd divorced their dad was because he struggled with homosexuality.

It was a shocking blow, but Leslie clung to her faith. When she graduated from high school she enrolled in a Christian college and continued her search for answers.

Two years later, while Leslie was visiting for her cousin's wedding, her father pulled her and Donna aside.

"This is really hard for me to tell you, but I'm sick," he said, his voice breaking. "I love you very much.... This is so difficult...but I am HIV positive."

Leslie's mind starting racing as her heart fell into her stomach. It was 1988, and the drugs that controlled the effects of HIV were years away. She knew HIV led inevitably to AIDS, and AIDS meant a death sentence. Beyond that, she couldn't seem to collect her thoughts.

She drove back to school in a daze, not sure if she was terrified, or hurt, or numb, or all three. "I was at Bible college—things like this don't happen. It was hard enough being one of the few with divorced parents, but now everyone would know my dad was gay."

Anger and hurt filled her heart, and Leslie started to lead a double life. She would be a good Bible-school student who loved God during the day, but then at night she would drink heavily with coworkers from her part-time job. She only slept a few hours at a time. The hatred in her heart was eating her up. *When would he die?* She was haunted by the question.

Leslie graduated and continued her fast-paced, alcohol-driven lifestyle. She knew her father was nearing the end, but when a family member called to tell her that he was in the hospital, she refused to go at first. She didn't want to have anything to do with him.

A close friend, Emily, finally convinced her that she needed to be there, and drove with her to the hospital. Leslie sat in the corner of her father's room, seething with anger and contempt.

When he tried to reach out and talk to her, she could only manage curt, two-word answers. She left as soon as he was stable.

But it was just a few days before he was slipping again, and the doctors said that it was time. Death drew near.

"I took the drive alone to try to come to grips with it all. By the time I arrived, he had a breathing tube, so he couldn't talk. I sat on the bed, looking into his eyes. He seemed resigned to die. For the first time, I took time to see the regret in his eyes, and I saw the love he had for me."

The hospital gave Leslie's dad morphine to make him comfortable as his organs struggled to function. They told the family he would pass quickly, but it took longer than expected. As his breathing became laborious, Leslie thought viciously, *Die, you worthless man!* She wanted the torturous last minutes to be over.

When he drew his final breaths, Donna sobbed. But Leslie could only stare.

"The funeral came quickly, and I was unable to hear anything the minister said about my dad with any kind of objectivity. He was saying words about my dad that described a different man. I thought Dad should rot in hell."

The guilt and shame of knowing she had wanted her father to die washed over her, adding to the pressures she already felt. She could hardly breathe at home anymore, so as soon as she got home after the funeral, Leslie packed her things and moved to another state.

In a new city, Leslie sank lower than ever. She drank more and more, slowly driving away her family and friends. Finally, only Emily, who had taken Leslie to the hospital to visit her father, was there for her. And eventually even she had had enough. She called Leslie to say good-bye.

"You are an alcoholic, and you need help," she said. "I'm

sick of seeing you waste your life away. I don't know if this is right, but I can't be your friend anymore unless you agree to get help. I can't deal with you anymore. You have to do it for yourself." Then she hung up.

Alone in her apartment, Leslie curled up on the floor in the dark. She knew Emily was right. She knew drinking wasn't going to fix her life. With no friends around, she finally turned to God. She realized that He had never left her, even though she'd done her best to leave Him.

"I began reading my Bible, and I exercised a lot to help with my anger. Little by little, I was starting to let people in. I sought out a Christian counselor and went a few times. It seemed to help, though I didn't enjoy it. Asking for help has always been a hard thing for me."

She started to take comfort in the words of James in the Bible: "Draw near to God and He will draw near to you" (James 4:8, NASB). And slowly, day by day, she found her way back. She learned to accept that Christ's blood covers a multitude of sins—not only her own, but even her dad's.

"I'm in a good place now. It doesn't mean I'm not tempted sometimes, but I don't allow myself to run away from God anymore. I now can consider that my dad might have made peace with God before he passed. I pray that is true. It doesn't matter if I think he wasn't worthy; what matters is the reality of God's mercy on us."

Hillary
Love Secured

*H*illary felt as if she never quite measured up. There wasn't one specific reason for her insecurities, but there were lots of small ones: she was adopted, bullies picked on her, her family moved, she wasn't popular, and she was overweight. She judged herself, constantly asking, *Am I doing the right thing? Am I good enough? Am I worthy of this?*

When she was twelve, she learned about Jesus at a local church. "After I was saved, things were better," says Hillary.

A young woman took an interest in her, becoming a spiritual mentor. Hillary grew in her faith—until her friend moved. "I kind of fell apart. The connection that had been helping me grow was suddenly gone."

When her dad started traveling for work, she felt like she was losing him, too. She took her hurt out on her mom.

"I started pushing my mom away. We fought all the time."

Hillary started dating. "I was fourteen; he was eighteen. I thought I was so cool—dating a senior."

One thing led to another, and Hillary became sexually active.

"My mind knew it was wrong, but I didn't stop because I was so excited to be in love." Her entire focus was her boyfriend. When that relationship didn't last, she found another.

Hillary couldn't deal with the disappointment in her parents' eyes. "I started running away, looking for love from older guys." That earned her a reputation at school. The popular girls wanted nothing to do with her.

"I was mad at myself and sick of my past." Hillary took her anger out on herself and attempted suicide.

Her parents took her for treatment at a private hospital, but the psychiatrist wasn't very compassionate. During one of her appointments, Hillary told him what she'd been doing. Angry and needing help, she thought he'd have the answers. He looked her in the eye and said, "You're a narcissistic little slut."

It confirmed everything Hillary already thought about herself.

"The only thing I learned in treatment was how to get away with more," says Hillary. "I learned to experiment with marijuana and then tried LSD. I liked it because it took me to an alternate reality where everybody loved me, and I loved myself."

But mostly Hillary felt worthless, undeserving of the love she craved. Before she turned eighteen, she ran away at least a dozen times. "I was running away from what I knew I was—a disappointment to my parents and myself."

Her plan was to lower the expectations of those who loved her most. "I figured if my parents didn't expect much, they wouldn't be disappointed. But I knew they were."

It wasn't that their expectations were unrealistic. Hillary was a smart and capable girl. But her insecurities and fears caused her to sabotage every dream her parents had for her. "I thought they'd lower their expectations. But they never did."

Her parents feared she wouldn't graduate from high school, so they moved her to a special school for kids who were learning-disabled and behaviorally challenged. Hillary thrived under the rigid structure, graduating with a 4.0.

Valedictorian of her class.

"Everyone was proud of me. I was happy." She stopped running away. A new psychiatrist helped her build self-esteem. He taught her that, even when she messed up, her parents still loved her.

On her eighteenth birthday, Hillary's mother wrote her a letter. "In the letter, she said she loved me even before I was born. She loved me the day they called and said I was theirs. When I was two years old and pitching a fit because my daddy was out of town and I wouldn't calm down until he called—she loved me then, too."

But there was more. Her mother wrote that she realized she couldn't make Hillary love herself or anyone else. She had been trying to dream for her daughter, but she wouldn't do it any-more. "You win," the letter said at the end.

Hillary wasn't sure what to make of it. On one hand, it affirmed her mother's love. On the other hand, her mom seemed to be letting her go, giving up. "She said she refused to continue fighting for the potential she thought I had. It really hit me hard, because she said good-bye."

Hillary admits she might have been happy to receive such a note, even though the message was conflicted, at fourteen. "But at eighteen, coming through what I'd come through, knowing I was still missing something and wouldn't find it in a boy, or even within myself—hearing her say good-bye was awful."

Hillary made plans to attend college in the fall. The day she received her admittance letter was one of the best days of her life. For the first time, she felt as if she'd lived up to expectations.

But when Hillary arrived on campus, she realized how unprepared she was. Her high school hadn't academically equipped her for college. Hillary dropped out.

A failure once again.

"I knew I couldn't go home. Besides, my parents were separated and my dad lived in another state. So I lived in my car, stayed with a bunch of idiots, and had a boyfriend who was a real jerk."

Camping one night at an illegal campsite, Hillary's boyfriend asked to borrow her car. Her best friend left with him, but Hillary stayed with the rest of the group. While they were gone, her boyfriend and her best friend had sex and then wrecked the car. Hillary didn't confront them when she found out. She just quietly cried herself to sleep.

She had nothing. No money, no place to live, no car, no friends, and no family. It was Thanksgiving week and it would be the first time her family didn't celebrate it together. Unwilling to spend Thanksgiving alone with her mom, Hillary called her dad. She begged him to send her a bus ticket to come see him where he was spending the holiday with her grandparents. He did. Her mom drove her to the station, and Hillary boarded the bus with nothing more than her purse and the clothes she wore.

Hillary stared out the dirty bus window, stained with the fingerprints of those who'd ridden before, for almost twenty-four hours. She stayed awake the whole time. The people on the bus had all lived hard lives. Like her, they were here because they didn't have other options. Some of them scared her. A few of them smelled. So did she.

Is this what my life has become?

She bummed cigarettes, exchanging them for her lighter.

I screwed up. I disappointed my parents again. I've cost them massive amounts of money paying for the cars I've wrecked, special schools, treatment centers, and college.

"I was terrified of what my dad would say. I don't think I'd ever been that tired." As the bus pulled into the station, she saw her dad waiting for her.

"He wasn't mad; he wasn't even disappointed. He was just happy to see me. I felt like I'd come home. I realized my dad and mom loved me. Until then, I thought my mom was just an overbearing pain-in-the-butt and I didn't see that for what it really was—love."

After that trip, Hillary made more mistakes, but she also made progress. No longer did she feel as if she wasn't worthy of her parents' love or that she had to earn it. She learned that, even if she disappointed them, she could still face them.

"That was one of the things Mom had always tried to get through my head. *I love you, but I hate what you're doing.*" That's what her letter had tried to say, but it took Hillary a long time to understand the difference.

A few years later, Hillary married a Christian man who knew about her past and loved her anyway. Together they started going to church, where Hillary learned that, like her parents, God had never stopped loving her.

"Looking back, I can see He never left me. He was always there. Between the ages of fourteen and eighteen, I didn't get any kind of weird disease, get pregnant, or get killed. He was the one who made sure I made it home safe. It wasn't through any of my own doing. Trust me—I didn't care."

Hillary still asks a lot of questions.

Am I following the path God set for me?

What are You teaching me?

God, can You help me?

In the past, her pattern was to run when things got tough. "I never stuck through the hard times because I couldn't do it alone. I still can't. But with God, even when things are crazy, He's strong enough to help me stick it through." Hillary finally found the love she'd so desperately chased, and, more important, the security to accept that love.

Ainsley
Escaping the Anger

Twelve-year-old Ainsley sat at the dinner table. She finished eating and started clearing her plate.

"Who's cleaning up this mess?" Her father spat the words in her mother's direction.

"I made dinner. You clean up."

As Ainsley cowered, her father picked up a plate and threw it across the kitchen. It hit the wall and crashed to the floor. He threw another one. Then another.

Her mom hollered back, standing up to him.

He grabbed her by the shoulders and threw her up against the wall as easily as he'd thrown the plates. He shoved her again. And then he dragged her to the bedroom. Ainsley heard muffled screams behind a slammed door.

Ainsley had met Jesus when she was three years old, when a neighbor took her to church. At thirteen, she made a public declaration of her faith, choosing to be baptized. She and her group of friends made a pact: they were going to be the "good girls" in school. No sex. No drugs. No cursing.

That was the year her parents divorced. Ainsley, a daddy's girl, wanted to move in with him. "He left my mother for this other woman, and she was not nice—very possessive and jealous of our relationship. At first my father would come and get us for visits. Then the visits turned into calls, and then the calls turned into silence."

Ainsley did not get along with her mom, though her mom attended every track meet, volleyball game, and school activity. Her mom struggled to make ends meet, constantly stressed. Tension rose between the two.

Ainsley ran away for a week. When she was home, she mimicked her father's rampages. She shoved her mother into the wall, hitting her. Once, she broke her mother's finger. Then she ran away again—another week away from home. She was living in a home for runaways when she talked to her mom. They argued about Ainsley's boyfriend, whom her mother did not like. Yet Ainsley still asked, "When will I be able to come home, Mom? You promised you'd get me out of here."

"You won't be coming home. I'm still not ready. We have a lot of issues to work through." She told Ainsley she'd arranged for her to live with another family.

Furious, Ainsley packed a small bag of clothes and fled the runaway house. She spent the first day in a camper adjacent to her boyfriend's house. The next week, she lived with his brother, then his sister. But her boyfriend decided he didn't want to be with her anymore and broke up with her. She began moving between the homes of various acquaintances.

Ainsley quickly learned to fend for herself. "I had no job, no money. I couldn't call my friends because they would rat me out, so I helped out as much as I could wherever I was staying for food and cigarettes. I would scrounge money I found lying around to buy things I needed. All I had was that small bag of clothes." Fear was a constant companion. "I never knew who was watching. I feared being caught and sent to another runaway house. I hoped I would survive another night away from home."

She worried she'd end up in juvenile detention, but she kept smoking pot. She couldn't go a day without it.

Her life as a runaway lasted four and a half months. Ainsley had no desire to return home, but on one rainy night, she was in a car accident. The policeman asked Ainsley for her name. She hesitated, and soon he found out she was a runaway.

Miraculously, Ainsley and her mom reconciled after her last runaway episode. "I finally appreciated her for always being there and always loving me, no matter what junk I had put her through. We became the best of friends."

During that time, Ainsley dated a boy whose family were Jehovah's Witnesses. Her boyfriend's father told her, "There's really no difference between Jehovah's Witnesses and Christians." He gave her materials to read.

In the midst of this tumultuous period of Ainsley's life, God sent her people who helped her find her way back. The first was Joe, the youth group leader in a church where Ainsley occasionally went with her mom. He saw the Jehovah's Witnesses books and asked, "What are all those books?"

"They're from my boyfriend's family. They're Jehovah's Witnesses."

"I see. And why are you reading them?"

"I'm interested in exploring something else, since God hasn't exactly been there for me, anyway."

"Ainsley," Joe said, "God never leaves you."

Ainsley was silent.

"You may not always like what He does or what He has you do, but He never leaves your side. Why don't you leave those books with me, then watch and see what God does to show you He's there?"

Ainsley gave him the books and started to pay attention. Slowly God began to show her the ways He'd been there all the time—physically protecting her through her parents' fights, the divorce, her drug use, and even running away.

As she was processing all of that, Ainsley's close friend was diagnosed with terminal colon cancer. "The very idea that you don't have to be old to die frightened me. Watching her battle cancer and seeing her faith allowed me to understand God through her eyes. I wanted to be as confident in my faith and relationship with Christ as she was."

But God used the smallest person to finally bring Ainsley fully to Himself: her daughter. She had been married for a year when God blessed her with Erica. "The birth of my daughter was one of the turning points of my faith. I was now responsible for molding and shaping a new life to love God."

Erica also played a key role in reconciling Ainsley with her father. After Erica was born, Ainsley let her grandmother know she was now a great-grandmother. Her grandmother called her father, who then called Ainsley. "At first I was angry! He wanted to see his granddaughter like it was his right. I was not going to allow him to break her heart. It took about six months of talking, praying, forgiving, hurting, and understanding before I actually let him come see her."

They reunited, but the experience felt awkward. "I was no longer this thirteen-year-old girl who was afraid to speak her mind. I was now a wife and mother who was confident."

It took Ainsley a year to open up to her father and let her guard down, but now she has a good relationship with him. "I am very grateful for the grace God has shown me through this process."

Once a homeless runaway, Ainsley is now raising two children in a stable, loving home. She has a college degree and works at her church. When she looks back on her prodigal journey, she smiles. "God has an uncanny ability to put the right people in my life. I was able to relearn how to pray, love, trust in the unknown, and follow the strength God gives. I was able to learn amazing lessons from the trials I faced. I believe those years have molded me into the person I am today."

Diana
Saving Herself

"M y mom was my whole life, my whole family."
Diana wasn't exaggerating. Her father was in and
out of prison for drugs, and on the rare occasions she saw him
he had his own issues to deal with. Her older sister and younger
brother were both half siblings with different fathers.

But Diana's mom was special. "She's the most inspiring
woman I've ever met. She was always fun. She'd get down on
the floor and play with us or take us to the beach. On weekends,
we'd hang out on Grandfather's boat."

Diana was in elementary school when her mom started having headaches. An MRI located the source of her trouble—a
large tumor wrapped around her mother's spinal cord. The doctors successfully removed the tumor, but her mother was par-
alyzed from the waist down. Confined to a wheelchair, she
couldn't play with the kids as easily. Life as Diana knew it
changed forever.

Her mother was determined to walk again, and over time
she was able to get around with assistance. During her recovery, Diana's mother heard the Gospel and accepted Christ as
her Savior and radiated an indescribable joy. It was obvious to
anyone who met her that her spirit soared.

Diana and her sister also accepted Christ. "I loved the Lord. I had this heart for God, and I really wanted to follow Him and do everything for Him," says Diana. For a while, everything was good.

But her mom's headaches returned while Diana was in middle school. They went together to learn the test results. Diana remembers sitting in the padded office chairs of the small waiting room. They kept their voices down as they talked and laughed, flipping through outdated magazines. But the conversation stopped when the doctor emerged, carrying medical files. He placed them in front of his assistant, pointed, and said, "Tumors."

That can't be Mom's file.

Diana watched the color drain from her mother's face.

It was. The cancer was back.

Diana's mother died a few months later, leaving Diana, her older half sister, and a younger half brother.

Diana's father didn't come to the funeral. But her brother's father came, and immediately took custody of his son. Within a week, they had moved to the other side of the country.

Diana went to live with an older relative a few hours away. Her half sister, a legal adult, stayed near their original home. In six days, Diana lost her home, her family, her friends, and the community she'd grown up with.

The next Christmas, Diana visited her sister and saw more than a sheltered teenager should see. "At the time, I only listened to Christian music. When someone cussed, I plugged my ears and hummed, 'Lord, prepare me to be a sanctuary.'" Her sister, on the other hand, had a lot of bad habits and no faith to speak of. Diana was shocked and worried.

Diana thought she could save her family. When she returned to her new house after Christmas, she announced that she didn't want to live there anymore. Though disappointed, her relatives let her go back to live with her sister.

At first, she lived with her sister and her sister's boyfriend in a trailer. Her sister didn't have a job, so Diana paid the bills with the Social Security checks that came after their mom's death. They didn't have enough money for what they needed. A counselor at school gave Diana food and toilet paper from the school's supplies.

Her sister was rarely home. "There was a shoot-out next door, and once, in the middle of the night, someone tried to break in while I was home alone." Eventually the counselor called Child Protective Services, and Diana was placed with another relative.

By now, Diana was no longer the good girl. She started huffing (abusing inhalant drugs) and smoking cigarettes. Before long, she was also smoking pot and using drugs. It took only a few weeks to become addicted to coke and meth. "It all happened so fast."

She started hanging out with older guys who could get her drugs. She lied about her age. She got her first kiss at thirteen from a guy who was twenty-three. Drugs were all she craved.

Gangs were all over Diana's neighborhood. Diana knew joining one meant access to drugs and parties, so she joined a group because one of their colors was red, and Diana had red hair. One night a guy invited her to a party, and she went with a friend. But when the girls got there, they realized everyone at the party was from the rival gang. The guys at the party sent all the other girls home, except for Diana and her friend. When she sipped the drink they gave her, she started to worry they'd put some kind of drug in it. She didn't know how to get away from the menacing partiers, but God continued to protect her. The police arrived a few minutes later because some neighbors complained about the noise, and she was able to slip out in the confusion.

Diana didn't live in any one place for long. She bounced around, staying with her relatives sometimes, or with her dad and some of his other kids when he was out of prison. One of her stepbrothers especially liked having Diana around because she could get free drugs from his friends.

Diana was in debt to her dealers, and they refused to give her any more drugs. Broke and cut off, she started the painful process of detoxing at a relative's house. "I stayed up for three weeks straight without sleeping. Then I couldn't move. I just lay in bed. I lost so much weight that when I started eating again, I gained twenty-five pounds in two weeks."

After a few weeks of this, Diana had finally fallen asleep at 3 a.m. when two strangers woke her, dressed her in clean clothes, and took her to a residential treatment center. Her family had finally sought help.

Since she'd already undergone detox on her own, the effects of the drugs wore off quickly in the center. Diana started thinking more clearly. "I felt God saying, 'Hey, Diana, I'm here for you. I've *been* here for you.' That's when I realized that even when I was the most alone, He was with me. He protected me from some scary situations. I never once prostituted myself, and I was never raped, which is amazing considering all I went through."

Though Diana was better physically, she still couldn't get things right in her relationship with God. It seemed she couldn't shake the spiritual cloud that hung over her. "I'd dabbled in Wicca. One day I mentioned it to the program director. Right then, she prayed over me to remove the dark things that had a hold on me. For the first time, I was able to breathe."

Diana began reading her Bible and praying. "A few weeks

later, a song came on at church and I knew that I wanted Jesus more than anything—even more than drugs. I went forward and fell on the altar. I prayed to God, telling Him that He was all I wanted and all I needed."

Her renewed faith helped her understand her past behavior. "I was trying to run and hurt Him purposely, like He'd hurt me by taking my mom and dad away." But Diana began to see meaning behind even the loneliest events in her life. "I understand my dad better now. And I may have lost my mom, but I gained other women in my life because I didn't have her. Though there's bad stuff, I see God's blessings in my life."

Diana moved back home after finishing the residential program. Today she attends a church she loves and is involved in a small group that holds her accountable. There are days she wishes her dad was different or her mom was still here. But as a child of God, she knows that no matter what, her heavenly Father will *always* be there.

part four

Friends

In the beginning...

Hagar

agar was a slave, taken from her Egyptian home and owned by the curious religious family of Abram and Sarai. It was not the ideal way to start a relationship, but the Bible indicates that, over the years, Hagar formed an unlikely bond with Sarai. She listened to Sarai's stories of the God of Abram, how He offered her husband surprising promises of offspring and becoming a mighty nation. And when the crisis came, we can imagine that Hagar felt the weight of their connection.

Hagar must have known she'd always be a slave girl, Sarai's handmaiden. She'd never be on the inside of Sarai's heart, never have a voice, never have the power to make her own choices.

But when Sarai said, "I will never bear children. Just look at me!" Hagar felt a pang of sympathy for the older woman. Her mistress grabbed Hagar's hand and placed it on her stomach, above her empty womb. "Can you feel any kicks? God plays jokes, Hagar. He says I will have a child, but I'm too old."

Hagar shook her head. "But, ma'am," she said, "God promised Abram a son. You told me." The God of Abram had become real to her. Here she stood, defending his God!

"I thought you were my friend." Sarai pushed Hagar's hand away.

Hagar didn't know how to respond. Friend? Yes, in many ways they were friends. They shared the same household, heard the same gossip, bore the same grief. But Hagar knew they would never have become friends if she weren't owned by Sarai. She worked in the inner circle because she'd been bought—certainly not wanted.

Hagar let out a long breath, steadying herself in the shifting tempest of Sarai's mood. "Yes, friends."

Something happened in Sarai's eyes, but she didn't smile. "You will prove to be the perfect friend. I must talk to Abram. Wait here."

Hagar milked goats while Sarai approached Abram.

"Now behold," she heard her mistress tell Abram, "the Lord has prevented me from bearing children."

Hagar stopped milking. She snuck nearer.

"Please go in to my maid. Perhaps I will obtain children through her."

Hagar sucked in a terrified breath. Sarai gave her away like a prostitute.

Hagar prayed a desperate prayer, hoping the God of Abram would hear her. She'd grown accustomed to Abram's prayers, had heard his steady voice move the heavens. Would God hear her if she steadied her voice? Would Abram see the futility of Sarai's crazed request?

But when she saw Sarai's eyes, she knew. Hagar hung her head, her breath escaping but only half filling her lungs.

Sarai grabbed Hagar's wrist and led her to Abram's tent like a lamb to the slaughter.

Hagar forced herself not to cry, but couldn't control her shaking.

"Here. Produce an heir." Sarai let go of Hagar, leaving her in the darkness of the tent with her master, who would soon be much more.

Once Hagar felt queasy in the mornings, she knew. Hagar, who'd been on the outside, now held Abram's child inside her womb. She, an insider! And at that, she saw Sarai as an outsider—a barren woman. She hated Sarai then. Her "friend" had never treated her as such, and now she returned the favor, stroking her belly, winking at Abram, shooting looks of contentment Sarai's way.

Sarai shouted at Abram, "May the wrong done me be done upon you. I gave my maid into your arms, but when she saw that she had conceived, I was despised in her sight. May the Lord judge between you and me."

Overhearing this, Hagar smiled. Surely Abram would find Sarai's claims ridiculous.

But Abram knew better than to get between two catty women. "Your maid is in your power," he said dismissively. "Do whatever you think is right."

Hagar saw the cold desire for revenge in Sarai's eyes, and she fled before something horrible happened. She'd been forsaken by her masters, and by their God, and now she had nothing more to do but oblige everyone and fade away.

She found a spring and sat down, caressing her belly, amazed at how much she loved her unborn child. She should never have risked her position by rubbing Sarai's face in her situation. She wept to think she'd never touch her baby's fingers, never look into her child's eyes.

A man appeared before her. "Hagar."

Her name! Who knew her name?

"Where have you come from and where are you going?" he asked.

"I am fleeing from the presence of my mistress, Sarai." Hagar hoped she'd find an empathetic ear, to pour her story at the stranger's feet.

"Go back, Hagar, and submit yourself to her authority."

This was not what she expected. To go back into Sarai's

world surely meant mistreatment and death—for her and her child. She said nothing.

"I will greatly multiply your descendants so that they will be too many to count."

Hagar thrilled at his words. This was a promise that she would live to see her child grow up.

"You will bear a son," the man confirmed. "And you shall call his name Ishmael, because the Lord has given heed to your affliction. He will be a wild donkey of a man, his hand will be against everyone, and everyone's hand will be against him; and he will live to the east of all his brothers" (Genesis 16:11–12, NASB).

How could He know this? Hagar must have marveled at the certainty in the speaker's voice, and found comfort in His words. In His knowledge. Over the years she had become accustomed to the mysterious appearances of Abram's God and His messengers, but to think that someone would come to her—a slave, a woman, a sinner who had made a mess of her situation.

Yet this stranger spoke as if he knew her. He saw her by the brook. He heard her. He sought her out.

A delicious feeling swept through her when she realized, all at once, that only Abram's God could know these things. He was appearing to her! Trembling, she said, "You are a God who sees."

The man left her, shocked and honored, there by the brook. "Have I even remained alive here after seeing Him?" she wondered.

Hagar returned to Sarai with a changed attitude. She no longer looked down on her mistress for being barren, but dedicated herself to her work and to raising her son to be the man God told her he would be. Sarai, for her part, allowed her slave to live with her husband's child.

Things were not easy after that—fractured relationships rarely heal without some scars, and Sarai's jealousy turned up again when the older woman unexpectedly fulfilled the angel's prophecy and gave birth to a son of her own. Once again Hagar was sent off into the wilderness. But this time, she cradled the hope that the God who sees would see her through. And He did.

Heidi
Living with Question Marks

*H*eidi grew up in a creative home. "We had the freedom to make tents in the living room, paint masks on our face with watercolors, and make up and perform plays all summer long." But when she was a teenager, her father worried that his children were growing up too fast and moved the family from the suburbs to the country. Heidi didn't feel like she fit into the new community, and she didn't like the rules her suddenly strict parents enforced on her. "I didn't like that I couldn't wear short shorts and miniskirts," she remembers, and she started to fight with her mom. "I took out everything I didn't like about my life on her."

Heidi started junior college looking for a fresh start. She tried church but found it boring. She went to a campus ministry group instead, where the student leader justified going to parties since Jesus hung out with sinners. Intrigued, Heidi found 1 Corinthians 9:22: "I have become all things to all men, so that I may by all means save some" (NASB). She wrote the date next to the verse in her Bible. "God was telling me to go party with the partiers," she says.

That Halloween she went to her first drinking party and tasted her first spiked punch. She wrote innocent letters home to her parents, but sent the real story to her younger sister.

Eventually, Heidi connected with a group of artistic students who chronicled their drug trips in a group journal that they passed around. "At first I would leave the room when they pulled out the bongs. I preferred drinking, which made me loud and uninhibited." She also knew being caught with drugs could get her into trouble. She stayed away. And because she saw how guys used her sexually active girlfriends, she didn't have sex. "I felt like the token virgin," she says.

But she enjoyed hanging out with her new friends, who filled a void in Heidi, particularly her need for community. She started to paint, remembering the artistic talent her mother had encouraged her to develop as a child. Heidi's paintings were different—dark explorations of the life she was living and the questions her heart kept asking about God.

"I felt like God was mad at me," Heidi recalls. "My lifestyle kept me away from Him. I would've liked to return, but I felt estranged, so I didn't."

She dated a guy, even though she knew he cheated on her. One Saturday, she found out he'd left for an off-campus party without her—a party that would last the whole weekend. Heidi was determined to go to the party, too, and talked a friend into driving her there.

Windows rolled down, Heidi felt free. The wind tossed her hair as her friend sped recklessly down the road. They met other cars full of potential partiers and started weaving in and out and around each other on a two-lane road. And then, a crash.

Heidi has no recollection of the accident, but she was told the crash ejected her from the car. She flew into a field and suffered severe head trauma, a ruptured spleen, a cracked pelvis, and a bruised lung. Her blood pressure was alarmingly low.

Heidi had to be airlifted to a large hospital. When her parents were notified, they jumped on a plane to be by her side.

A gifted cardiovascular surgeon diagnosed Heidi's blood pressure problem as a torn aorta. He operated for twelve hours. When he came out of surgery, he said, "It was my hands, her heart, and God during the surgery."

Though successful, the surgery was not without complications. The hospital replaced Heidi's blood more than four times. For days, she lay in a coma, only to wake up with amnesia. She spent a week in ICU. "I woke up in a hospital bed, my arms tied to the sides, my left leg in traction. My mom was in the hall, but I went back to sleep," she recalls.

Consciousness rolled in and out. Friends visited. "I knew that I knew them, but couldn't recall who they were or how I knew them. One read *Jonathan Livingston Seagull* to me and remarked about the bald spot on my head."

Most of Heidi's memory returned, but the last year of rebellion became a blur. She stayed at the hospital for five and a half weeks while her broken pelvis healed. She spied a Gideon Bible on the nightstand and began reading it. "I read the book of Romans, and God used a verse to break through a lie I had believed that kept me from Him. It was the last verse of chapter 10, a quote from Isaiah: 'But of Israel he says, "All day long I have stretched out my hands to a disobedient and contrary people" (Romans 10: 21, NKJV). All of a sudden I saw God with His hands outstretched, no pointing fingers. He wanted me back. I needed to know that."

Her father's unconditional love in the hospital pushed Heidi forward in her journey back to Jesus. "He helped me. He was just happy I was alive." And through her recovery, he gave her a surprising gift from a strict father—grace. "My dad didn't ask questions," she says. "He simply loved me where I was."

Though she wanted to return to school once she could walk again, Heidi's recovery was too slow for that. Her words still got mixed up when she talked. "I was walking with crutches, wearing a medical corset, and I had a shaved spot on my head." Her neurologist told her to rest, not to return to school for six months.

When she was ready, Heidi transferred schools. She knew she did not want to return to the crowd she'd hung out with before.

At her new school, she connected with a dorm Bible study and got involved with a campus ministry. This time the leader didn't encourage students to hang out with the party crowd. Given a new chance, Heidi started to live a new life, designed to please God.

Heidi kept one of the pictures she'd created during her rebellion—a black canvas full of question marks. She sees it as a testament to the lengths she ventured away from God, the hopeless place where she ended up, and the lengths He went to woo her back.

Carrie
Searching for Acceptance

C arrie grew up knowing God had given her a gift of music as a songwriter and singer. She heard God clearly through song, but she didn't always know how to deal with what He told her. Carrie felt most comfortable when she was making music, and she served wherever there was an opportunity—church, coffee shops, recording studios, and county fairs. Music was a vehicle that allowed her to focus on Jesus, to forget the problems around her, and to strengthen her faith.

Her music led her to Rick, who was also a Christian musician. They began dating, and it quickly became serious. Rick proposed after only a couple of months.

The happy couple played their music at a number of Christian events, and Rick talked openly about how great God was. He told her he believed God had a wonderful plan for them both. So Carrie was shocked when Rick broke off the engagement three days before Christmas. He had been seeing another woman, a mutual friend of theirs, for several months.

Carrie was beyond devastated. "If this is what Christianity is like, I don't want anything to do with it." She turned her back on her Christian community and moved to a new house, got a new job, and took up marijuana and alcohol to numb the hurt.

She worked at a diner, where she endured men's lustful looks in exchange for good tips. She used the money to support her growing drug habit.

A regular crowd of bikers often filled the diner. One in particular, Joe, paid a lot of attention to Carrie. She was attracted to him, but tried to avoid him because she knew he was married. Carrie had not forgotten how it felt to be cheated on, and made it clear she would not do that to another woman. However, she flirted with him for months, until one day she found out Joe's wife walked out on him.

Joe and Carrie moved fast. He moved in with her, and within three months, Carrie was pregnant.

As she spent more time with Joe and his friends, she discovered that the group of bikers was actually a gang. It made Carrie nervous to think about bringing a baby into a violent lifestyle, but she overlooked it. These were her friends. For the first time since Rick left, she felt truly accepted. Here were people who were as angry as she was. In her wildest dreams, she never imagined she would find "family" in a gang, but she found herself wearing a biker rag and their gang patch to declare she was their property—part of the family.

Parties were rough. Men waved guns around to show off. The relationships were all about power and intimidation. Crime was rampant, and talk centered around violence and stories of who they beat up. Carrie felt as if, somehow, this way of life was honest and these people loved her, and so she convinced herself it fit her personality.

After Julia was born, Joe became distant. Carrie worked late nights, and he was unemployed on and off. They began to argue, and then their fights became physical. Carrie pleaded for him to leave her alone, but he wouldn't. Hurt and afraid, Carrie started to sleep on the couch.

She knew she needed a change and that she couldn't rely on Joe. She wanted more than this for her daughter. Tentatively, Carrie started going to a Bible study to see if God could fill the void. Most of the time, she was high or drunk, but the Christians just kept loving her. Church became part of Carrie's life again.

After a couple of months, she made the decision to get clean—no alcohol, no drugs. Joe didn't like the changes. After one particularly vicious fight, Joe yelled, "Just leave, Carrie!"

She packed one bag for Julia and one for herself, and left.

The emptiness made her wonder if she could ever love again. She cried out to God. Sometimes her prayers were full of anger; sometimes she confessed her brokenness.

Carrie's pursuit of God grew more intense as she realized how much she needed real love. After putting Julia to bed one evening, she turned on the radio and collapsed after a hard day. She found herself taking in the words of a love song about finding true love. God spoke lovingly to her heart through music again, saying, "Now I can finally be your true love." Carrie fell asleep sobbing.

It took Carrie a while to physically and financially recover from her tumultuous time with Joe and to be able to support Julia and herself. At times it seemed like she was in a constant battle, taking two steps back and one step forward. But within a year, she had a car, an apartment, and a good job. She even decided God was leading her to enroll in Bible college. The days were long, but Carrie's hard work paid off.

She felt like she was in a good place a few months later when she saw Joe for the first time since their breakup.

"I found myself crying over feelings I couldn't understand. But the feelings weren't about my broken heart—they were about bitterness and rage. I wanted to hurt him like he had hurt me, emotionally and physically. . . . I prayed, 'God, where are You? Did You leave me because I walked away?'"

Carrie felt God's answer come gently and lovingly. "I was right on that couch, where I knew you would go when you were ready to come back."

When she allowed herself to embrace His grace once again, she discovered the power to forgive. Through prayer and humbling herself before God daily, Carrie was able to let go of all the pain and anger toward Rick and toward Joe. She no longer needed it as a wall of protection around her heart.

In celebration of her new life, Carrie threw away everything associated with her gang life. She loves leading her church in worship, where she encourages others to always listen for God's voice. She knows God is greater than fear, anger, and sorrow, and that the most powerful experience can be found in singing His praises.

Robin
Mirroring the Popular Crowd

"I was insecure," says Robin, looking back at her high school self. "I was consumed with being popular, and being popular took a lot of work." Robin spent an hour straightening her hair each morning. She always wore the right clothes and regularly went to tanning appointments. When Robin looked in the mirror, everything was right—her looks, her clothes, even her friends. She was happy, or at least she told herself she was.

Being popular meant Robin had friends—but it didn't mean they were the right ones. Robin's Christian parents were protective and wouldn't let their teenaged daughter hang out and party the way the other kids did, but Robin found ways around their rules.

Her parents were sound sleepers. After they went to bed, Robin would sneak out the basement door and walk around the house to the road, where her friends would pick her up and take her to the biggest gathering. When the party broke up, Robin's friends took her home. She'd sneak back in through the basement door and return to her room. Her parents never knew she'd been gone.

She started dating Max, an older guy from the neighborhood. Max drank more than most of her friends, and a lot more than Robin. She wanted to make him happy, make him think she was cool, so she started to drink more to keep up. It made her feel grown up.

But one night at a party, Max had too much to drink. He started an argument with Robin, raising his voice and getting out of control.

Then he slapped her.

Robin didn't react. She hated conflict, and if someone stepped on her, she'd let him do it again. "I wanted to make him happy, and I didn't want him to get mad again," says Robin. The next time they went out, she drank as much as he did. "I didn't want to think about what was happening."

One very drunk night, instead of sneaking in the basement door, Robin staggered up the front steps, rattling the door as she tried to get in. When she finally made it inside, her parents were awake and waiting. They found their daughter smelling of alcohol, with wet hair and clothes. They accused her of many horrible things that night; some she'd done, some she hadn't—but she let them think it was all true. "It wasn't as bad as they made it out to be," says Robin, "but at that point, I didn't care what they thought. Let them think the worst."

Her parents tried to crack down, but they couldn't stop her. "I became a monster," says Robin. "I did things I'd promised myself I'd never do. I gave my body to guys to keep their love. I was superficial and materialistic. I yelled at my parents to make them hurt like I hurt." She started partying all night and not coming home. The former A-student started failing classes and didn't care.

Robin didn't recognize the sad girl in the mirror. "I'd go to bed miserable. I wrote poems about suicide. I'd lost myself."

At a friend's party, Max drank ten beers before Robin stopped counting. On the way home, he was so drunk he couldn't steer the car, and Robin tried to steer from the passenger seat. They made it home, but it terrified Robin. A girl from the same party, who had drunk only half what Max did, hit a tree on her way home and died instantly. For the first time, Robin acknowledged that her behavior could kill her.

"I knew I needed to change. I hated myself. I had more friends than before, but I was also lonelier than I'd ever been. I knew what my heart was missing," Robin says.

Robin started attending youth group activities at her church. During a weekend retreat, the pastor talked about holding a mirror up to see who you really are. He asked them where their relationship with Christ was right then, on a scale of one to ten, and where they wanted it to be. Robin wanted it to be a ten, but when she looked in the mirror, she knew it was more like a two.

Robin craved God's love and acceptance, but didn't feel as if she deserved it. "There was no way I deserved God, not after everything I'd done." When others walked forward to make a decision for Christ, she stayed in her seat, crying. She knew she'd missed her opportunity.

Later that night, a friend called. He'd seen her crying and wanted her to know that God loved her just the way she was. He reminded her that Jesus forgave all of our sins. That night she accepted Christ as her Savior. "It felt as though the fog had cleared, the curtain had been pulled back, and I opened my eyes to see the light shining through the darkness," says Robin. "I was changed, and I wanted to live a changed life."

But it's hard to be a new creation in the same old environment. "I wanted to tell all my friends what had happened. I wanted to say, 'Listen, we should all be like this,'" but her friends didn't want to hear it. "My friends wanted the old Robin back." And she wasn't strong enough to resist them.

Robin started to slip back into her old partying patterns, but this time her parents were ready. They interrupted her down-fall and sent her to a program for troubled teens. She cried until she couldn't cry anymore, and then she started praying. "I knew God was with me, and that He would give me the strength to make it through."

In Robin's program, clothes were no longer a personal state-ment; they were issued by the program. "We had these ugly jeans and T-shirts. We couldn't wear make-up or do our hair. The things I used to hide behind were taken away. All I had left was myself."

Her days consisted of five hours working on the farm—"I'd never even seen a goat before; I thought it was some kind of a dog"—and five hours of homeschooling. "I didn't want to do any of it. I was a piece of work," says Robin. Each girl had to work through several levels of trust before they were allowed to leave.

Robin's path wasn't direct. It was filled with starts and stops. For the first four months after she was admitted, Robin made very little progress. "I'd get so far and then I'd screw up and lose my level." She had to learn everything the hard way. But as time went on, she channeled her anger into her work. "I would work harder, run faster, and do more than anyone else. It became a fire in me."

She also learned she could lean on God. "As I watched girl after girl lay abuse, rape, deaths of fathers, deaths of mothers, STDs, drug addictions, problems with the opposite sex, and problems with the same sex at that small country church's altar, I saw Jesus take it all."

In Bible studies, Robin learned more about God and His Word. She also saw His love demonstrated in real and personal ways. "The staff loved us all so much, and no matter what I did, they saw the best in me. That's what finally made me want to become the best I could be." It also helped her understand that that's how God saw her.

"Piece by piece, like a broken mirror, I gave myself to Him. The more I gave, the more I healed. That's when I realized who I really was." Robin worked hard to graduate from high school a year early and became a leader the other girls looked up to.

Today when Robin looks in the mirror, she doesn't see that old insecurity, or even the broken fragments of someone she hates. She sees hope and a happy brown-eyed girl who wants to change the world for Christ.

But one thing hasn't changed.

She still sees someone who cares about what her Friend thinks. Only now, she's friends with God first, and His opinion is the only one that counts.

Cate
Releasing Her Devastating Secret

*F*our-year-old Cate had a loving Christian family, and her childlike faith was already growing. "But by sixteen or seventeen," she says, "I thought boys just didn't like me. The good guys would laugh and joke around with me, but never ask me out. I started to think I must be a lesbian. I hated that and didn't want it, but I felt like it must be my doom."

At eighteen, wholehearted in her faith and her desire to serve God, Cate left home to be a full-time missionary with a youth missions agency. She led short-term mission trips and spent most of her time training others. But even though most of her students were close to her age, all the guys were off-limits. "There were lots of dating restrictions," she says. "We weren't allowed to date students at all, and the guys I could date weren't asking me out. Again I felt weird, like there was something wrong with me. That's when I met Sheri. We had an immediate bond and became deep friends very quickly."

The two young women did everything together. They had other friends, but those friendships faded because Cate and Sheri were always hanging out. One summer they traveled together with people they worked with, driving a van around the country to promote their organization. "We were together all the time," Cate says. "We ate together, spent our days in the van together, camped all around the country." During that trip, the girls' relationship became physical. "I hadn't planned for that or expected it to happen; it just kind of did. I think I was open to it because of all my insecurities. I wanted a relationship. I wanted someone to love me."

It was the beginning of a devastating secret. Cate and Sheri hid their relationship because they knew they would be kicked out of the group and face public humiliation if anyone knew. "I knew it was wrong," Cate says, "but it felt like the only thing I had. I didn't know what I would do without it. I think I felt, too, like I was doing something good for [Sheri]. I was loving her and supporting her and being there for her." Cate kept going to church and kept working full-time. "I led mission trips but felt like I was going to hell. The foundation of my Christianity was rotting away with guilt."

While the relationship gave Cate something to hold on to, it also cut her off from everyone around her, plunging her into painful isolation. "Our other friends didn't really want to be around us because we were so close," she says. Someone within the organization did confront the girls, but they were able to talk their way out of it. And when Cate worked up the courage to seek advice from an older woman, the woman promised to follow up with her, but never did.

"I was miserable," she says. "I knew this was something I shouldn't have had, but I didn't know how I would survive letting go of it."

The relationship continued off and on for several years. When Sheri said she was thinking about moving on for good, Cate plunged into depression. "I would go into the bathroom and cry for hours. I couldn't stop." She started cutting herself and wearing long sleeves in the summer to hide her scars, secretly hoping someone might realize what was going on. When Sheri finally left, Cate was completely broken. "It was the most difficult time of my life. I was so conflicted. I wanted to hurt myself, even though part of me knew I didn't really want to die."

Yet in the midst of the grief and pain, there was repentance. "It was a process," she says. That spring after Sheri left, Cate spent time alone, crying to God, processing her feelings. "I knew God was changing me. I began to feel like there was hope. I don't think I was capable of taking big steps, but I wanted to obey the Lord, and I was able to obey in very small things." One of the steps Cate knew she had to take was to talk to her mom. "I didn't confess everything, but I started to share with her. That was a *huge* step. I think that day part of my heart opened to allow God in."

Eventually, Cate was able to talk to her mom about more of what had happened, and her mom met her with love and grace rather than judgment. "Talking to my mom helped me get closer to God," she says. "She's like my God-catalyst on earth. She accepts me where I am and doesn't embarrass me, but at the same time, she challenges me to grow."

Now Cate's heart has been made whole again by the grace of God. Her burden of guilt is completely gone. "God saved me from hating myself," she says. "I've never hated anyone like I hated myself."

Cate is hesitant to offer advice based on her experience, but she says, "I would change my story if I could. Most of all, I would encourage people to know that God still loves us when we disobey. Pray for a willing heart and seek advice from someone you trust—if not your parents, find a friend or mentor. Don't keep it inside. The thing that will hurt you the most is keeping the secret. You know, when I look back, I think whatever embarrassment I would have suffered by talking about what was happening would have been worth it. It could have saved me years of pain."

Cate moved back home and spent a wonderful, healing year with her parents. She got involved in a church and now meets weekly with her pastor's wife for mentoring. And she became good friends with David—another healing relationship, which eventually grew into dating. While they've struggled with the sexual aspect of their relationship, they've both been able to repent and move forward—and they're not keeping secrets. Cate's mom is helping her stay grounded and is holding both of them accountable.

"I think God sees every little effort you make," Cate says. "If you can only take one small step back to Him, He'll help you take the next ten."

Allyson
Distanced from Love

Allyson came to Christ when she was eight years old. Her parents took the family to church nearly every weekend, and Allyson's relationship with Jesus was strong. In junior high, Allyson loved youth group and dragged her friends to church. She was popular, and her non-Christian friends respected her. She was the "real deal," never succumbing to peer pressure but, instead, demonstrating through her life what a close relationship with Jesus looked like.

On fire for God, she enrolled in Bible college after high school. She met Bryan, fell in love, and was married in her early twenties. It should have been a "happily ever after" story, but things got messed up after that.

"We had some pretty serious communication and expectations issues," Allyson says ruefully, "and it just seemed to me that marriage was not turning out to be what I had expected."

She and Bryan were both busy with their jobs and lives. Allyson started to confide her personal trouble in a coworker, who was "safe because she didn't know Bryan. But the more she talked about it, the worse the situation seemed to her. This was the first time she had verbalized her pain to someone. "Looking at it from where I am now, my wandering heart, though I didn't ever have an affair, was caused by resentment toward Bryan....I thought we would be closer and happier together. I never thought marriage could make you feel so alone. I know Satan took advantage of me in that state of mind, and helped me turn my resentment and anger toward Bryan into immature actions in the world."

After Allyson and Bryan had their first child, a son, their relationship grew even more distant. Bryan spent much of his time at home in front of the computer, often leaving Allyson to eat dinner alone while he took his plate back into his office. Love felt like a distant memory. Feeling abandoned, Allyson continued to confide in friends, and in particular a divorced woman named Madeline. The two women hung out a couple of times a week, commiserating over how the men in their lives had broken their hearts. Madeline's husband had cheated on her and left her for another woman, and her anger impacted Allyson. Their resentment became a familiar friend.

Before long, Allyson's innocent evening trips with Madeline to run errands or go to dinner turned into late nights at dance clubs. Allyson had never been a drinker, but she found a few drinks that she liked, "to be sociable." And with those drinks came poor decisions.

The unspoken bar rule was that, if you were there, you were "looking." It didn't matter that Allyson wore a wedding ring; men were constantly coming up to her and Madeline and offering to buy them drinks or asking them to dance. For the first few weeks, Allyson always said no. After a while, though, she thought, *What's the harm? It's just hanging out*. But the dancing and talking soon led to more. Allyson could not believe some of the conversations she found herself having with guys.

"I can't say my troubled marriage made me turn from God completely," she says thoughtfully now. "But enough that I had the wrong priorities, and I created enough distance to do what I wanted. I still had my faith, and none of this was a real deal breaker with my belief in Jesus. I didn't question who Jesus was to me, but my struggles with Bryan did have an effect on my evening plans."

Allyson felt alive again. The dancing made her feel sexy, and complete strangers were obviously more interested in her physically than her own husband was. She loved the combination of alcohol and attention. The only hard part was that Bryan never seemed to be bothered by the late nights. He didn't call to check up on her, and they still didn't talk when she was home. Bryan would ask what she had done the night before, but she thought he didn't seem to care about the answer, so she didn't tell him the truth.

Somewhere under all the bad behavior was the Christian girl who used to witness to her friends. Allyson still knew, at least in theory, that God was right there with her. She knew He was watching her in the corners of those bars, which was what kept her from having a full-blown affair and leaving Bryan. "I didn't keep going to bars just because I knew I could get forgiveness from God, regardless of how I'd partied the night before. It was more like I knew God understood my pain, and that He would be waiting for me whenever I was done."

Finally, though, the double life got to her. There wasn't one particular minute or event that shook Allyson's life. Rather, there was a steady stream of small voices and nudges from the Holy Spirit that Allyson had a harder and harder time ignoring. Finally, she couldn't. She acknowledged the conviction to stop going out, to stop drinking, and definitely to stop flirting with other men. She knew she was called to concentrate on God and on the issues she had in her marriage.

Allyson had to confess to Bryan what she had been doing,

which wasn't easy. But they agreed to work on their marriage and acknowledged that the eventual solution was out of their hands. Only God was in control, and His plan was the only thing that could bring two broken people together.

Allyson is in a better place now, even as she struggles with her relationship. Allyson and Bryan continue to have issues, despite Christian counselors and a renewed focus on God. Allyson's honest conclusion is, "The closer I am with God, the more loved I feel! The more time I spend in the Word and in prayer and in ministry serving others and my husband, the more content I am, even though my marriage isn't where I want it to be. Bryan and I are going to make it because Jesus is in our marriage, too."

Jackie
Lonely No More

Sixth grade marked the beginning of middle school—and of an oppressive loneliness that would haunt Jackie for years to come. She had a few acquaintances, but no friends. The rich kids at school cared about material things, but Jackie didn't have the kind of stuff or take the kind of vacations that would impress them. Shy Jackie ate by herself at lunch and tried to stay in the background, afraid of being seen as an easy target. She was lonely and sad in a way that she now recognizes to be clinical depression. Darkness covered her once-sunny life.

Perhaps if she'd had one close friend during those formative years, her entire story would be different. One peer who cared could have steered her away from some of the decisions she made later. But in sixth grade, Jackie thought she was alone. When someone she trusted started to sexually abuse her, there was no one to tell, and a horrible pattern emerged that would repeat itself over the years.

"I don't know where I got the idea," she says today, "but I started cutting myself. It seemed to make me feel better. Then in ninth grade I developed anorexia and bulimia. Satan was filling my head with lies—and I think he always knows which lies we are most likely to believe."

Tenth grade marked a new kind of rebellion—Jackie was drawn to the punk rock crowd in school, where she finally found people who felt like friends. She started wearing all black, dyed her hair purple, and shaved part of her head. At least now, she felt, she had a group. She belonged.

"I went to church and youth group and had a few friends there, but I don't think I ever knew how to apply Christianity to real life. I felt like God wasn't cool, and I didn't know how to make my Christianity work at school."

In spite of seeing Christian counselors, Jackie's depression deepened. Her arms, legs, and stomach bore self-inflicted scars she tried to hide. After graduation Jackie left for college to get out of her parents' house, since she fought with them all the time. But living on her own, she stopped going to class and slept most days. She wanted nothing to do with God. She was smoking and drinking, experimenting with drugs and sex, and not eating. Jackie flunked out of school after the first year.

Jackie's parents loved her and couldn't watch her kill herself, so they sent her to a Christian program that would help her recover from the anorexia and bulimia. She didn't want to go, but knew she had to in order to put off the fear of being alone. "It was terrifying, but I didn't want to be out on the streets." Jackie rebelled against anything Christian, but went along with the program, doing what she had to do in order to get out.

The loneliness followed her back home, and Jackie started looking for a guy to rescue her. She found Paul, who treated her badly. She cried all the time, but she desperately wanted someone to hold on to, someone to pull her out of her own life, so she married him.

Paul left her for another woman after a year and a half, thoroughly breaking what was left of Jackie's heart. "I had built my world around him," she says. "I had never felt so alone in my life. I told my parents, 'You need to do something or I'm going to kill myself.'"

Jackie received professional help to get over the worst of her depression and suicidal urges. In the mental hospital, wanting to die, Jackie listened to her mom tell her that God would never abandon her. It was a turning point—a piece of hope in the midst of the horrible darkness.

Jackie and her mom started taking long walks in the middle of the night. "I had to get out—and she would flood me with Scripture. I had nothing left, but I started to pray. I felt as if I were going to jump out of my skin, and God was telling me, 'Be still, and know that I am God.' While it was very painful, there was something happening—a stilling of my soul. There were other verses that came back to me from my childhood, like 'Trust in the Lord with all your heart, and lean not on your own understanding' (Proverbs 3:5, NIV). I had to hold on to that belief or I would die."

Jackie started dating an atheist, who challenged her beliefs during their long conversations. "He made me think a lot and made me start defending my faith. I knew I shouldn't be in this relationship, but my discussions with him, in a way, made my faith grow stronger."

After a lot of prayer, Jackie knew she had to decide between him and God. "I *had* to choose God—I had to. I didn't want any more of 'what Jackie wants.' I wanted what God wanted for me." For the first time since sixth grade, Jackie chose to be alone. She started doing in-depth Bible studies and prayed for God to show her His true character. She found a Christian counselor who helped her work through her difficult past and replace the lies Satan had told her with the truth of God's Word. She started once again to feel loved by God.

At a local community event, Jackie ran into Alex, an old

boyfriend from high school. Jackie was nervous about getting back into a relationship—she didn't want to waste any more time or make any more mistakes—but she could tell there was something different about Alex. Together they pursued God, who led them to marriage.

Jackie finished her degree and became a teacher. She and Alex are raising his son and continuing to pursue their love relationship with each other and with Christ.

"I'm light-years away from the girl I used to be," she says. "I have only recently really realized how God loves me. I mean, I've always known He loves me, but I guess I thought I had to do something to earn His love. He told me through a song that it's not because of who I am that He loves me, it's because of who He is. Even when I pushed Him away, even when it was so dark that I felt like I was in hell, He was there, waiting for me to return—encouraging me to return—with open arms. He left love notes along the way, wooing me back to Him. I'm sorry it took me so long to notice them and to respond, but now I know to look for them. I often ask Him to remind me that He loves me, to show me how much He loves me, to hold me close and comfort me, and to whisper words of love to me. And He does!"

Shannon
Matched by Grace

*"Where were my parents and Christian leaders? Did
they really not notice how I was dressing at church and
what I was advertising? Didn't they notice that the crowd I
was in didn't love God?"*

Shannon looks back at her high school life now with regret.
"The world hooked me in to its sinful culture, and no one
said a word to me before it was too late.... I think my parents
were just as scared as I was."

Her story didn't start out that way. Shannon grew up with
Christian parents who were very involved in church. She doesn't
recall praying a prayer for salvation, but she loved God from
her earliest memories. Without anyone really explaining it, she
knew He was her Savior. He would be the Someone she could
depend on.

But Shannon was lonely, and her heart began to wander. She
felt as if her Christian parents didn't have time for her. Shannon wished they would plan to do things together as a family
instead of sitting in front of the TV every night. She wanted to
talk about God, but those conversations never happened.

Around junior high, Shannon began to develop relationships with a new set of friends. She started trying to fit in—"a little smoking here and there, just to be cool." These new friends did not go to church or know about God. But they seemed to care about her and wanted to spend time with her, while her parents and her youth leaders were in their own worlds, "serving."

Painfully, Shannon recalls the breach. "I began to further distance myself from my family. My relationships with boys always centered around the physical touch I craved from my parents. I was still in youth group, but only to get out of the house. My group leader and I didn't connect at all, and she didn't know what to do with me. I couldn't talk to her. There was just no connection there." When Shannon's mom asked the youth leader to spend more time with the troubled teenager, Shannon felt like her parents were just passing her on to someone else.

This was the opportune time for the enemy to come in and begin to speak lies about Shannon's life and who really loved her. The line was drawn in her heart, and she separated herself from the Christian life she had known and started to live with a substitute: the world and the love it could give her. Her friends nurtured her need to be accepted, while the Christian community made her feel invisible.

Shannon found herself alone. "That was a hook in my heart that pulled me deeper and farther away from God. My parents weren't telling me not to care what others thought of me. I wonder how different my life could have been, had I known not to seek the approval of others."

As she continued to walk closer and closer to the "wrong crowd," Shannon stopped and looked to see if anyone in her family recognized where she was headed. She couldn't understand how her parents were missing all the signs exclaiming, "I'm in trouble!"

Ultimately, Shannon knew her choices were just that—choices. She couldn't blame anyone but herself. Her clothes were seductive, her music was explicit and crude, and then there were the boys. Shannon was only fourteen when she first had sex with her boyfriend. By the time she was seventeen, she had slept with almost thirty different boys, some in their twenties.

"When my mom found out I was having sex, she yelled at me and told me my boyfriend was just using me for sex. She was right, but because I was fourteen and had just given my virginity away, the words cut me to the core.... My new friends weren't welcome at my house." Shannon looked for any excuse to get out of the house.

"I spent my time outside of school drinking, smoking, and having sex with anyone and everyone who showed interest. I was an easy catch for boys—and men. Having a boyfriend was so important to me...finding someone to love me. It became easier and easier to be with anyone. If a guy said he wanted to have sex, it was totally fine with me. I was living dangerously and losing my soul."

This resulted in the darkest time of her life. Life was quickly spinning out of control, and she didn't recognize herself anymore. To cope, she ventured into the drug scene. What began as a once-in-a-while joint became an everyday pot habit. Continually, Shannon looked for ways to numb the painful reality of where her life was headed. All along, God knew her need. "Ironically, when I was stoned was when I felt a tug on my heart to return home to my First Love. God was graciously reminding me that the seed He firmly planted was still in my heart. But my guilt kept me away," admits Shannon.

Life at home became more rules, more guilt, and condemnation. So many times she found herself feeling too dirty to turn to God. The truth was, she didn't want to feel the embrace of another guy. She wanted to feel the shelter of God's arms around her. But she wasn't sure how to stop this horrible cycle of sin, how to find the way home. At the end of her strength, Shannon looked around at her friends and their lives—and she knew she wanted more.

"At nineteen years old, I got married. Really, I am not sure why. I knew I did really love Rich, but I think I married because I wanted to feel safe and secure in a relationship and find my way back to God. Having a husband gave me stability. For the first time in years, I felt God working in my life. I knew my heart was damaged, used, and abused. God was the One who could clean up our house . . . and He has!"

Shannon's pastor told her that grace is the empowerment to do what you cannot do on your own. Grace for Shannon was realizing she needed God to make marriage work, and grace came when God showed her the beauty of a committed relationship.

"God has taken an ordinary person, a sinner like me, and given me a job to do—that takes grace! No devil or demon in hell was a match for God's plan."

part five

Man Trouble

The Sinful Woman

he Bible doesn't even give her a name. She is called only "a woman who had lived a sinful life" (Luke 7:37, NIV). Her sin is not identified, but in those times, the sins that would brand a woman for life had to do with men. Sex outside of marriage was not easy to accept or ignore back then.

She was probably a prostitute, or perhaps an adulteress. Either way, she had given in to temptation and used men—or been used by them—to live her life outside of the shadow of God's love. She'd made bad choices, and she knew it. Her heart was bruised and battered, torn up by the behavior of the men in her life, who at one point may have seemed like protectors and providers.

She'd heard the gossip spreading through Galilee about a different kind of man, a gentle rabbi who was talking about forgiveness and reaching out to the outcasts He met—people like her, who could not find forgiveness in the temples or the town centers.

She found out that a local church leader, a Pharisee named Simon, had invited Jesus to dinner. She wasn't an invited guest—those meals were only for men, and even if they weren't, no one would invite someone with her reputation. The men of her village were willing to visit her in the dark and use her to satisfy her needs, but there was no way they were going to be seen with her in public.

But she had to go, to see the great teacher everyone talked about. She had to find out for herself if He was really as kind as they said. And if so, and if she could just get near Him, perhaps He would be kind to her. How long had it been since a man had reached out to her with anything but lust?

So she went to Simon's house, and slipped into a shadowed corner of the room. She watched the honored guests come in, sit down, and start to eat. She was surprised at how quickly it all happened—there was none of the ritual washing and anointing that Jewish men offered to their most honored guests. No one came and wiped the dust from the feet of the rabbi or helped Him clean up. They were not rude, but they were obviously not as excited about this man as she was.

We don't know what Jesus said at the beginning at that dinner, or what happened to draw the sinful woman out of her shadows. But whatever it was had a powerful effect on her. She'd always had a weakness for men.

As she got closer, tears welled in her eyes. As she heard His voice, she must have remembered all the reasons why she was called a sinner. She must have been overwhelmed by the things she had done with other men. At some point, she must have seen that *this* man was different. He did not see her for her body. He represented love.

When she reached Him, she was weeping, and her tears fell on Jesus' feet, still dirty from the long day's walk. Plenty of men had made her cry before, but not like this. And so the sinful woman, already looked down on by everyone in the room, humbled herself even more. She uncovered her hair and used it to dry the dust and tears from the rabbi's feet. She even kissed Him a time or two, which was a sign of reverence and respect. She was overwhelmed by the knowledge of her own sin and the feelings of peace radiating from the man before her. She was oblivious to everyone else in the room.

When most of the dust was removed from Jesus' feet, the woman took another daring step and removed the personal vial of perfume she carried with her. She started rubbing the scent—her chosen scent—into Jesus' feet.

It may have been the smell of the perfume that finally alerted the dinner guests to what was happening. The spiritual spell that had drawn her to Jesus was broken, and suddenly she felt all the cold, disapproving eyes in the room turn toward her.

Men had been her undoing, and they weren't going to let her forget it now. They saw her reputation, not her tears. She was a woman of sin, and she was taking great liberties with their guest. And He didn't even seem to mind! What kind of prophet was He, Simon wanted to know, if He didn't even know what kind of woman was touching Him? Because surely He wouldn't allow a woman with a reputation like hers to get near Him.

Jesus, of course, knew all about the woman's sins. He'd known them before she drew near Him, knew about her before He'd ever set foot in her town. But He also knew what the other men at the table did not know. He knew that her tears were her repentance. He knew that her sin was in the past, and that her foot-washing had been the most heartfelt, public commitment to a new life that He would experience in that room.

Simon, a church leader, had welcomed Jesus into his home and had engaged Him intellectually. But he had not put his heart into it. He had not lavished honor upon his guest the way the woman had. Perhaps it was because he believed that he didn't need forgiveness. He wanted to get to know Jesus, but he did not *need* Him the way this sinful woman, abused and ill-treated and alone, did.

Jesus looked right at her and publicly forgave her. And in that moment, the "woman who led a sinful life" experienced Jesus' love in a way that only a prodigal returning from the edges of hell could feel. She had fallen further than any other person in the room, and so her return to God's love was that much sweeter.

She'd been drawn into sin by men, and forgiven by One as well.

Amanda
Living with the Consequences

May 15 I haven't told anyone that each time I stand up I feel like I'll faint. Is it my blood sugar levels or is it that? I don't want to worry Shane or Mom, so I'll keep quiet and pray to God—I don't know what to pray.

*A*manda first understood that sex was about more than making babies when she was in sixth grade. Her dad had recently become a pastor at a large church, and the family had moved away from the small congregation where Amanda grew up. But after they moved, Amanda's dad confessed that he'd had an affair. He told the leaders at their new church, and then Amanda's parents shared the news with the kids.

Amanda saw the ugliness of church politics through her family's struggle. The church fired her dad. Most of the people from their old life abandoned them as well.

Church had been Amanda's whole life, and losing that community hurt her deeply. As her parents spent a lot of time rebuilding trust in their own relationship, Amanda unintentionally fell through the cracks.

Amanda met Shane when she was fifteen and he was sixteen.

As their relationship grew, the young couple signed a True Love Waits contract with conviction. They said they would draw their line at holding hands. But after a few months of dating, Shane kissed her. Things went faster physically after that.

Looking back, Amanda knows that "we fell in love way too young, and I was very vulnerable to affection. My faith had been worn down. My dad's affair caused me to be disillusioned with God. It seemed as if the church wasn't there for me during the hardest time of my life—I felt a huge void in my heart."

Amanda started to fill that void with Shane. The physical temptations grew, and their relationship suffered. They had a hard time trusting themselves to be alone together, so they broke up out of frustration many times.

They got older, graduating from high school and starting college together. And finally, they caved in and bought condoms from the vending machine the first weekend they were on campus.

May 19 It's almost day 34. Shane held me and told me, "It's all right to cry. I don't mind—cry. It'll be okay." Oh, what if I am pregnant? I probably am. Now what? This is no fairy tale.

Shane and Amanda broke up after they had sex for the first time because they knew the relationship could not go back to what it was before, and it couldn't continue like that without being married. With four years of college left, neither of them was ready for marriage.

While Amanda's conscience had bothered her all along the way, it wasn't until she finally gave herself to Shane that she realized how double-minded she had become. It was painful to have such an intimate relationship without the reassuring commitment of marriage. "I couldn't talk to anyone about my heartache, because I was acting like two different people." Instead of filling a void, her dependency upon Shane only created a bigger void in her heart.

Amanda found herself back in Shane's arms five months later, when three of their friends tragically died within weeks of each other. "We used one another for comfort in a storm of loss and confusion," Amanda explains. But their reunion became far more bonding than they expected. Their relationship was sexual again, and this time there were bigger consequences than a breakup: Amanda got pregnant.

June 10 Today I found out for sure that you are inside of me. I don't want you to hear or see me crying. I don't cry because I've hurt God. I love your father so much and he is my best friend. He loves me and I am his best friend, but at this point I don't know if God has our hearts prepared to marry each other. I have felt from almost right away that he is the one for me... the one who God sent to love me.

They knew their own love could not get them through this. They knew they needed to turn to God. Diligently, they sought advice and encouragement from those they looked up to spiritually. Through restless prayer, painful discussion, and help from others, Amanda and Shane decided that the best thing for them to do was to get married after all—not because of the baby, but because their love and commitment were real.

July 19 Oh, child, what I will do for you! Your father and I have put off the wedding date again! Not by my choice. Your daddy is struggling to find a job with benefits. He wants to go to school, too. He feels 19, I guess. I don't think he believes he can possibly provide for us. I don't know how to feel. I just hope you never have to know this pain. Would you want to stay with me if your father and I don't get married for a while? What if we never do? I cry because I am overwhelmed with the consequences of my sin.

"We both cried at our wedding because we felt such a release from the fight of our flesh. Our ceremony was more to us than celebrating our bond of marriage—it was a public commitment of our desire to completely surrender our lives to Christ."

No one ever wants to get caught. But Amanda believes it was God's grace that she was exposed through something as physically apparent as an unplanned pregnancy. Because her sin could be seen by everyone, she was forced to let go of her pride. After being humbled, walking around with a growing tummy, she had nothing to lose. "My stuff was out there for others to judge me. I had no choice but to work through it. God didn't desert me during this time; instead, He built me up."

Amanda and Shane are still married and raising their family together. Amanda is quick to tell others, "I take full responsibility for my actions. I know God brought Shane and me together, but He never wanted us to be so dependent on one another. His grace was such that, even when I walked away from Him, He waited for my return. Once I returned, He took my mess and made it more wonderful than anything I could have ever dreamed for myself. Today I live truly free!

"I am a prodigal daughter. I could have taken the narrow path, but instead I chose my own. Thankfully, once I saw where I went wrong, God brought the narrow path back around and connected it with my own path. He made a way. It looked impossible, but He did it. Though it radically disoriented me for a time, it came together in a more beautiful way than I could ever imagine.... Now that's grace!"

Ashleigh
Slipping Through Her Fingers

Ashleigh grew up in the church her parents had always gone to—the church where they were married. While she didn't feel a deep connection with God, she knew Jesus was her Savior and that He loved her. She gladly took a True Love Waits vow at sixteen, and at twenty-five had kissed exactly one boy, one time. She started to feel strange and left out. "I was sure I was the only virgin my age who wasn't a virgin just because she took a vow," she says, "but also because she never had the opportunity. I was frustrated that my plans for marriage and kids weren't taking shape. I was lonely and beginning to fear that, in fact, God didn't love me after all and was holding out on me."

As Ashleigh's bitterness grew, her faith deteriorated. "There was no life-changing moment where I decided God didn't exist—it was more of an eroding of my heart, so tired for so long, expecting so much but having nothing. I felt as if I had been asleep for seven years of my life." Unable to go on teaching something she no longer believed, Ashleigh resigned from her job as her church's youth director.

She had no desire to go to one last youth camp in the mountains, but it was her final task; then she could walk away.

"I didn't want to be there," she says. "You know, the goody-goody smiles, the worship services, the team-building games. I was exhausted and empty. It was all an act for me at that point."

For the first few days Ashleigh resisted. She purposely shut down, not wanting to listen to anything. But the third night, the speaker began to talk about Barabbas, the notorious prisoner who was released before Christ was crucified. "He talked about how each of us is Barabbas—how each of us was released from our punishment when Christ took it on our behalf," Ashleigh says. "In that moment, I felt the Holy Spirit speak to me. I knew I had been forgiven. I knew Christ was real. I can't explain it, but after all the drifting-away I'd done over all those years, God reached down and, in that one moment, changed my heart. He brought me to my knees."

Ashleigh's spirit was renewed. She spent quiet time by the lake in the mornings, looking out at the beauty of the mountains and talking to God. She rededicated her life to Christ and began studying His Word, worshiping Him with all her heart. She was on such a spiritual high, she never imagined she could be in danger. And while she didn't realize it then, she may have taken pride in her new spiritual state, setting herself up for a fall.

At a concert, she ran into an old friend. She'd heard stories about Chase's rebellion in college, and together they celebrated their return to faith. They started to talk and hang out. Soon they got together every day. Then they were out too late on Saturday nights to make it to church on Sundays. "I knew I loved him," Ashleigh says. "I still loved God, but I stopped worshiping Him and started worshiping my friend."

Ashleigh and Chase started drinking together, making their way through a six-pack or twelve-pack in an evening. After too many late nights at his house, they became sexually active. "It just kind of happened," Ashleigh says.

This friendship that had started with a spiritual connection had become warped and unhealthy. "I wanted him so desperately," she says, "but he was never sure he wanted me. So for six months we ran in circles—hang out, have sex, regret it in the morning, vow never to do it again. I started trying to support my behavior with Scripture, even though the Bible is definitely against sexual immorality of any kind. I was a mess."

Because she no longer sensed the Holy Spirit speaking to her heart, Ashleigh tried to convince herself that what she was doing wasn't that bad. But there was simply no joy left in Ashleigh's heart. She couldn't smile. When she wasn't with Chase, she was crying. When she was with Chase, she drank until she could forget about the situation.

Ashleigh borrowed the DVD series of Beth Moore's *When Godly Women Do Ungodly Things* from her church and went through it on her own. She knew she had a choice to make, and she knew what she had to do—to start respecting herself, to obey God. She promised God she wouldn't sleep with Chase anymore. "I was sad, mostly because I knew I was giving Chase a free pass to leave me and that he would take it, and because I could feel my dreams of a husband and kids in the near future slipping through my fingers."

Two weeks later, they planned to meet for dinner and a movie. But when Ashleigh made it clear there would be no alcohol and no sex, Chase canceled. He had a date with someone else.

Ashleigh was devastated. "Even now, talking about how brokenhearted I was makes me sad. I gave so much to this man without even realizing it, and I lost myself along the way. I sinned grievously. I was ashamed."

But God had plans to bind Ashleigh up and heal her wounds.

"God is so amazing. And He loves me so much. He helped me sort through my tears and broken heart and mended it. There are scars, because He had to perform some major surgery, but I have never been as close to my Savior as I am at this moment. I remember actually feeling Him hold me through one night of solid sobbing. I was the prodigal son, and there is nothing like feeling His acceptance upon returning. I thought God loved me before all this, when I first realized He was real and pursued a relationship with Him, but I had never felt it more fully demonstrated than during those months after I came crawling back to Him, used and spent."

Shortly afterward, on a visit to her sister's, Ashleigh was full of questions about what she had done and what God would do with it. Had she wasted two years of her life? Quietly, Ashleigh listened to her heart and was assured that God could take even these mistakes and use them for some eternal purpose. "I don't think God wants us to sin so we can grow," she says, "but He also doesn't waste our experiences. I think this whole relationship with Chase helped sift some things out of me—my lack of self-confidence, my dependence on other people. Those got me into this situation; now I understand how dangerous they are, and I've grown in both of those areas. And I understand God's love now better than ever before."

Ashleigh gets emotional talking about the love of God. As the tears start to fall, she says, "God lavished His love on me. I have hope. Because God loves me so much, I can be healed completely. I can't even describe how good I am doing right now. And I'm humbled, because I know I have so much more to learn."

Ashleigh now works with the women's ministry in her church, sharing the hope of the love of God with other women.

"Sometimes I still question God's plans for my life," she

says. "It's something I'm working on. But I know He has my best interest at heart. And He has shown me that I don't need a boyfriend or a husband to love me in order to feel complete. He's all I'll ever need. And that is love enough. His unfailing, lavish love."

Sarah
Traveling the Valley of Temptation

Sarah grew up in a small Midwestern town where neighbors were friends. Church was her life, her culture, and her framework.

When Sarah was in high school, she attended a retreat with her youth group. It was a three-day weekend where teens and young adults came together and spoke about dying to self and taking up one's cross to follow Christ.

"I remember one message in particular that was delivered by my friend Ron, who is now an evangelist. He spoke about a Scripture in Matthew that said that the road to destruction was wide and many would go that way. Then Ron read another in Revelation about how God wants us to be either hot or cold, because if we are lukewarm, He will 'spit us out of His mouth' (Revelation 3:16). Something very strange happened while he spoke. My heart began to beat uncontrollably, and I was sure everyone could hear it. A nervous feeling gripped me. Thoughts about not being completely sold-out for Christ tortured me."

Her sins began to play over and over in her mind until she came to the realization that she was not good enough to get into heaven. Her lifestyle and choices were not "hot" for the Lord and did not please Him. Even though she had been living a relatively good life, she knew it wasn't a sold-out life. A groundbreaking thought struck Sarah. Going to church because you didn't know anything else was not "it." Doing church work was not "it." Her parents' faith and all of those prayer meetings were not "it." She needed to make her own decision to follow Christ. All the way for Christ!

When Ron's older brother started a church in her area, Sarah joined the team to help build the new community.

She became very close friends with one of the pastors, David, as well as with June, an older woman who also worked at the church. "June, David, and I did so much together and were really good friends. But my relationship with [David] gradually became too close. We were spending a lot of time together [working], and then just the two of us, alone." The problem was, David was married and had a family already. "I found myself making many subtle choices to be with him, even though I sensed that the Lord was not pleased with this new closeness in our relationship."

During a gathering at the church, God spoke to her out of nowhere, *Leave the meeting and walk home.* She knew then that He was warning her about this relationship, and she could not lie to herself anymore about what was going on. She knew the Lord was asking her to break ties with David. *But I am doing good things working here,* she told herself. Yet it wasn't the whole truth. With conviction, she got up and walked out.

David was speaking to the group when Sarah left, but he stopped and asked everyone to wait while he actually followed Sarah out the door. He called her back, and even though she knew the Lord was telling her to just walk away, she went to him.

"Sarah, I'm in love with you. Please consider pursuing our relationship. I'm sorry for my feelings, but please...consider what we have."

Sarah knew that what he was asking was horribly sinful. In the mist of the angst and drama, she could feel the Lord asking her to choose between this man and Himself.

"I found in that moment the realization that I was actually in love with David, and that I had chosen him in a hundred little ways—a hundred little ways that had led me far away from the safety of the Lord. I stood there and chose him, my pastor, who was a married man."

Even though Sarah tried to stay away from David, her heart drew her toward him. She could not find her way back to the intimacy she once knew with Jesus. As the relationship became physical in the following days, she struggled deeply with all she had been taught and all she had come to know and believe about Jesus Christ. "I was struggling with being so emotionally attached to this man. I convinced myself I couldn't walk away. How could God ever take me back when I knew what I was doing was wrong?"

Sarah avoided her family during that time so that she wouldn't have to lie to them about her relationship with David. She became isolated from friends and stopped going to social events. The only reason she kept attending church on Sunday was so that no one would become suspicious.

"All of my life up to that point, I had been instructed by my mother to save my heart and my body for the one true love Jesus would bring me to be my husband. I had nice boyfriends in high school and kept my heart guarded. I knew my virginity was nothing to give away. It was easy to wait for marriage, because I knew God's design was best. I was excited and anticipated His model for love. My mom always told me that if a man asked for sex outside of the bonds of marriage, he didn't really love me. He didn't really want God's best for me."

Sarah and David drove around in her car, talking about how

wrong their relationship was. They talked about running away together, but Sarah would always end up suggesting they break it off. They spent a lot of time kissing. But Sarah drew a line and would not have sex with him.

"I was shocked when he asked if we could have sex. I knew that meant stepping even farther away from Jesus, more than I already had. That was my wake-up call to come back. I broke off the relationship. I knew I needed help."

David was supposed to be Sarah's spiritual mentor, but she could not turn to him for help. Finally she turned to her best friend, Linda. She told her everything as she fought back tears. Linda was shocked, disgusted, and very upset with Sarah. And when Sarah saw and heard her reaction, she was confronted with how sinful the relationship really had been. Linda's response was clearly out of love for Sarah and was another wake-up call for her.

Sarah knew she also needed to confess to June, who was so hurt by what Sarah had done that she could barely speak to her. Their close friendship was severed.

Through all the confrontations that followed, the Lord was right there with Sarah. He didn't need any proof of her repentance, and she took great comfort in knowing He knew her heart. He was directing Sarah through a vicious storm she knew she'd created. Because of God's grace, Sarah grew closer to Jesus in that time than she had ever been. Relationships were damaged all around her, but Jesus began to fill her and heal her. As painful as it was, she extended her hand over and over to those who chastised her. She was learning about real love and the cost sin can have.

"I know my story is a familiar one to many young girls. I've talked to many girls and women who also have been involved inappropriately with pastors. No matter what, God is faithful to work out any mess we create for ourselves. When you know you have received such undeserved grace, it is so much easier to give it away to others. He is always there, ready to save us from our sin. No one has to remain estranged. His children can always turn around and come running home. It's the real kind of love."

Tammy
Discovering the Real Thing

ammy knew her family loved her, but as the youngest child she felt alone and unappreciated. Her older brothers were successful and smart, and Tammy could get lost in the rush.

"Do you know what I think?" Tammy would ask, trying to break into the family's dinner conversation.

"No one cares what you think," a brother would reply. And her parents let him. Tammy learned to eat without speaking.

Tammy's family attended a traditional church, which was unusual in her liberal community. Tammy and the three other Christian kids at her school would be mocked for their faith. Because she was so scrawny, the bullies occasionally hit and kicked her, calling her "Bible thumper!" Most kids just looked the other way.

"I felt sad, really sad," says Tammy, who never retaliated with physical violence. Her faith ran deep, and her convictions were even stronger. She endured the taunting and the beatings and continued to share her faith.

But as she grew, things began to change. Physically, Tammy started to fill out. No longer the gawky girl, she was now becoming an attractive young woman. She'd also learned a few things about evangelism. Instead of preaching to the kids at school, she invited them to hear speakers on controversial subjects. "I was friendlier, spent more time getting to know people, and I became more approachable."

As Tammy invested in relationships, others invested in her. Suddenly she found herself in the center of an ever-widening social circle. Kids from school started coming to her church. But it wasn't just her faith they were interested in. Tammy noticed she was also attracting the attention of the opposite sex.

One of her most persistent pursuers was Luke. Like an eager puppy, he'd show up at her house to do homework. "He wouldn't leave," says Tammy. "He kept asking me out and he wouldn't take no for an answer." It didn't take her long to say yes. Though she'd never dated a non-Christian, she was flattered by his attention.

After a few group outings, they started going out alone. Soon kissing led to touching. They even talked about getting married someday.

Tammy knew dating Luke went against everything she believed, but she found ways to justify it. *"Unequally yoked" isn't really a biblical principle about only dating Christians,* she told herself. *It's just an old-fashioned phrase that's lost its meaning.* Besides, she really liked Luke. He paid attention to her, laughed at her jokes, and made her feel special.

One night, after a few drinks, Tammy felt more relaxed than usual. Instead of stopping with kissing and touching, she let things continue. Tammy slept with Luke.

It was a line she'd never intended to cross. "I knew I'd done wrong," says Tammy, but her feelings overwhelmed her logic. *We're going to get married, so it doesn't matter. Besides, God forgives sins. He'll forgive this, too.*

Tammy thought she'd finally found the love she longed for.

But that one night became a pattern. Soon she was lying about where she was and what she was doing. "I felt divided. I knew what I was doing was wrong, yet I was still doing it." Tammy lived a double life. "I knew God loved me, but I couldn't feel God's presence. Luke was right there in front of me."

Tammy's friend Carol saw what was going on. She'd been in a similar situation and had spent a year as a short-term missionary, getting her life together. She suggested that Tammy do the same. Tammy had done missions work in Europe before she met Luke, and she always thought she would go into Christian work full-time. Perhaps this was what she needed. "The idea of going into the mission field had been haunting me for some time," says Tammy.

It didn't mean she and Luke were finished; in fact, they still planned to marry. Before she left, they picked out a gold ring, and Luke placed it on her finger. The ring would be a physical reminder of his love.

The first two weeks of Tammy's training focused on knowing oneself and knowing God. For some, this meant dealing with unresolved sin in their lives. The group sessions were designed to break down the new missionaries and rebuild them in the image of Christ. "I knew it was going to happen. I lied to myself, saying I'd go and listen to it all and still go back to Luke." Tammy thought she'd be a good missionary while she was there, and then go back home and continue sleeping with her boyfriend.

Until she met someone who changed all that.

"I'd always believed in God's grace. He was a lovey-dovey, fuzzy God who would let me do whatever I wanted and forgive me for it later." But that year Tammy met the God of the Bible. Through a series of speakers, Tammy came to know God as an awesome Creator, not just as her forgiving pal. She met a God who required commitment and obedience. "For the first time I saw a different reality. I realized God didn't *have* to love me, that He could choose to reject me—He's that big. I realized I needed to honor and respect Him in a way I had never done before."

During those initial weeks of teaching, not only did God get bigger in her mind, but so did her own sin. Sex before marriage wasn't part of God's plan. *Can God still love me after all I've done? After I disobeyed Him?* "I started to feel sick about what I'd done. I wanted to go drown myself in the lake in front of the building, I was that upset," says Tammy.

She knew what she had to do. Nervously, she picked up the phone and called Luke. She wasn't sure how he'd take it when she told him she was breaking up with him. But before she could get the words out, Luke surprised her. "Tammy, while you're away, is it okay if I see other people?" Though it was what she needed, it hurt to hear it.

Tammy poured herself into her missionary duties after the breakup. "The forgiveness I felt was real," she says. She began to experience God in new ways. He provided for her financially, and she witnessed miracles and incredible things. God was physically present for her in a way that even Luke had never been.

As Tammy learned more about the God of the Bible, she made changes in her life. "I surrendered finding a husband. I didn't care if I was single for the rest of my life. I never wanted to betray and grieve the Holy Spirit again."

In a gift shop, Tammy found a gold ring with a cross. She took it out of the velvet box, fingering it slowly under the shop lights. Tammy knew what she wanted to do. At the next group missions meeting, she told the leaders there was something she wanted to say. In front of everyone, she took off the amber ring Luke had given her and gave it to one of the leaders. Then she took the gold purity ring out of its box and slipped it onto the same finger. It seemed to shine even more brightly than it had in the store. Though it wasn't intended as such, that meeting became a commitment ceremony. Tammy vowed to wear the purity ring until her wedding night. She already saw God working in her life, and now she had a symbol of His love.

Looking back, Tammy says, "I think Luke was a fake savior. I was looking for God's love, but I was distracted by a physical decoy." Tammy's faith, tested through all those years in school, gave her the strength to turn from her sin. Her purity ring became a tangible reminder of the Real Thing.

Kelly
Meeting God

*H*er grandfathers were ministers and masons, shepherding the church and building it brick by brick. Even with that history, Kelly didn't have a personal relationship with Jesus.

When she was a young teenager, a local businessman named Frank spoke at career day and handed the students his business card. Kelly wrote him a letter. Frank responded by taking her under his wing. He approached Kelly's mom and asked, "Could Kelly go away for the summer? I'll pay for her to go to Bible camp." Her mother agreed. And there, surrounded by other young Christians, Kelly gave her heart to Jesus Christ.

Kelly dedicated herself to Jesus and to sexual purity, and suffered the social consequences of her convictions. In high school, she dated popular guys who would take her out, then never call her again because she wouldn't have sex with them.

But things changed for the better when she met a friend of her brother's. Her brother said, "I don't want this to happen; it might turn sexual," but Kelly knew she was strong in that area.

On one of their dates, her new boyfriend told her, "I don't want to have sex."

She thought, *Oh perfect!*

But soon girls at school pulled her aside, sharing their stories of her boyfriend's sexual escapades. "He wanted to marry a virgin," Kelly says, "but he said he had these urges that he had to satisfy now."

They ping-ponged back and forth, Kelly taking him back when he said he was sorry, then pushing him away when he had sex with someone else. Eventually, during college, they decided to get married, setting a date to shop for an engagement ring. When she went home one weekend to visit him, she noticed that a young single woman in church was holding a baby in her arms.

That baby looks like my fiancé, she thought. She confronted him and was heartbroken to discover that her suspicion was true. They broke up for good.

At that point, Kelly said, "I give up." It didn't seem to matter if she stayed pure. Kelly found a new boyfriend whom everyone thought was perfect. He was thoughtful and kind. He noticed her tattered Bible and gave her a new one for Christmas.

Man, he really gets me, she thought.

He continued to shower Kelly with gifts. In the spring he told her he loved her. But after his declaration of love, he told her, "We can't be together because you're a virgin."

She didn't want to let him go, so she gave in. "I was so stupid. Of course, I didn't see that then—only when I thought about it later."

He assumed that after they'd had sex, she'd move in with him without getting married. But she put her foot down. Instead, she moved back in with her family, working full-time and taking care of her parents and siblings.

Kelly floated in and out of long-term relationships, waiting, waiting, waiting for that magic marriage question to be popped, but it wasn't forthcoming. "I saw all my friends getting married. I should have had more faith in God to see their blessings as signs to me that my day would come. Better yet, if I were never to marry, I should have had faith that God knew best for my life."

A guy friend she'd known for a long time came back into her life, just as the despair over still being single was sinking in. He didn't want to mess around with dating. Since they'd known each other for so long, he reasoned, they should just get married. And they did. Everyone seemed happy about the union—her parents, his parents, and Kelly, too.

Until her husband started blocking the door.

He didn't like Kelly going places without him. He monitored her activities. And when she wanted to go out with friends or attend a local Bible study, he stood at the front door, barring her exit. The only way she could get out of the house was to call her father to come and get her, because her husband wouldn't make a scene with her father there.

But he caught on to her trick of asking people to come over so she could leave the house. One day she picked up the phone and it made a funny sound. He'd had the line blocked so she could only make emergency calls. He showed her his cell phone. "If you need to make calls, you come through me first."

He used to like weekly dinners with her family, but now he started to discourage her from attending. Her father noticed the increasingly controlling behavior and pulled Kelly's husband aside. They talked about anger, and her father encouraged him to go to counseling. Kelly hoped things would be better.

But when she came home from Bible study one evening, her husband sat in the darkened living room, a knife and a gun in his lap. "If you go back to church," he said, "I will kill both of us." Kelly was terrified.

Not long after that, a girlfriend invited Kelly out to dinner, and her husband agreed to let her go. At the end of the night, instead of returning home, she drove directly to the police station, then to a battered women's shelter. It was there that she had the marriage annulled and found out she was pregnant. The day she found out about the baby, a priest came to the shelter for his monthly visit.

"Now that I knew I was pregnant, I felt bad that I had ended the marriage. I didn't want to bring a child into this world without a father, so I realized I'd have to go back to this man." She shared all this with the priest, explaining that going back was her punishment from God for having sex outside of marriage.

"The priest didn't make me feel bad. He said I could be the mom my baby needed without remarrying this man. And I'd seen enough of *Oprah* to know what would happen if I went back."

"God will be the baby's Father," the priest told her.

Her business mentor, who'd paid for her to go to camp so long ago, encouraged Kelly as well. "We will all be the baby's fathers," Frank told her.

"I thought I could only return to God if I married my baby's abusive father, but these two men helped me see that I could return to God just as I was, even with my child. I felt I had to get married to be good, but they told me I could be good alone—with God's help."

So she returned to God, laying her life at His feet. She gave birth to Angelique after months of extreme health problems. Hospitalized for a long time, sometimes so weak she had to maneuver through life in a wheelchair, Kelly started to build her life again.

Today Kelly owns her own business, and her health has improved. She regrets that she didn't choose the best father for her daughter. "[Angelique] is the best thing in my life. I wish I would have chosen someone who would treat her like the princess that she is, someone she could see God moving through.

"When you come back to God," Kelly says, "He restores your life." Kelly spends her spare time encouraging teenage girls to wait on God. She tells them, "It's very, very hard, but you will not regret it."

Suzanne
Removed from Her Transgressions

Suzanne didn't look like a prodigal daughter in the making. She accepted Christ as her Savior when she was six years old, in the church where her father was a pastor. Her parents divorced a few years later, which was hard for Suzanne to accept, but she threw herself into her youth group and grew even closer to Jesus.

At a youth rally in ninth grade, Suzanne heard Rebecca St. James's song "Wait for Me" for the first time, and she made a public commitment to save herself for marriage. She dated a guy through high school, a committed Christian, and they kept their pledge of abstinence. But when they broke up, Satan knew just how to tempt Suzanne.

After two years at Bible college, Suzanne moved back to her small hometown and sang on a worship team at her church. She started dating a guy who also volunteered at the church. They looked like a strong, God-centered couple. Suzanne's friends cheered her on and encouraged her to throw herself into the new relationship. In those first idyllic months, it seemed as if Suzanne had met her Prince Charming.

But there were cracks under the surface. As Suzanne started to get more serious about her boyfriend, she started to feel uncomfortable singing on Sundays. Something in her heart didn't feel right, and her voice didn't sing praises the way it used to. Her music pastor noticed and asked her if something was wrong. Specifically, he asked if she and her boyfriend were having sex.

They weren't, and Suzanne said so. But her pastor had recognized the danger lurking. Less than a month later, Suzanne gave in to the temptation and had sex for the first time. And in that one decision to turn away from God's will for her life, everything changed. Suzanne got pregnant.

Going to her parents was difficult, but admitting the truth to her pastor was heartbreaking. He accused her of lying to him. How could she be pregnant less than two months after she told him she wasn't sleeping with her boyfriend?

The pastor's disbelief and the whispers and rumors that surrounded the young couple in their own church drove Suzanne's boyfriend away from God. Angry, he started to look for friends and fulfillment somewhere else.

Suzanne was torn. "I knew I had messed up, but I wanted my child to know Jesus," she says. "At the same time, I wanted my relationship to work. Abortion was never an option." Faced with the disapproval of her church family and her own lingering sense of guilt, Suzanne turned all of her attention toward her new family. Her boyfriend started to spend the night at her apartment more often, but they didn't get married.

She stepped down from the worship team but continued going to church alone. "I wouldn't say I ever left God," she explains. "But I was making a lot of choices that weren't of God. I was numb to what I was doing." Every Sunday she would stand with the congregation while the music played and cry silently. She had lost her heart for singing.

After her son was born, Suzanne did everything she could

to stay with her baby's father. She poured her heart into him, making compromises and overlooking his lies and bad behavior in order to give their son a complete family. She didn't want her child to grow up with separated parents the way she had. But nothing worked. While Suzanne's heart longed for a family, her boyfriend wanted the freedom of single life. There were lots of fights and even more tears. Their friends got involved, trying to help but making it worse instead.

Then, in the middle of the turmoil and when her son was only a few months old, Suzanne got pregnant again. This time, her boyfriend made it clear that he didn't want the responsibility of a family.

Suzanne's mother tried to help, giving her books to read about unhealthy relationships. Both of her parents stood beside her through five years of her tumultuous relationship, loving their grandchildren and encouraging Suzanne to once again seek God's favor, instead of her boyfriend's.

Finally one night, as she packed both babies into the car to go looking for their father, who had lied about where he was, Suzanne broke down and let the words she had heard seep into her soul. As she drove, Suzanne began to pray out loud.

"How do I get out of this mess?" she pleaded.

"Move." God's voice, silent for so long, was so clear that Suzanne almost drove off the road.

Once she heard God, there was no stopping her. She broke up with her boyfriend, ending the toxic relationship for good and giving her heart back completely to God. She started to sing again. She arranged for a job transfer. She called pastors in the new city and found an apartment. And with her parents' blessing and her friends' support, she moved forward into a new life.

It wasn't easy. Suzanne's children were still babies, and she was alone in a city where she didn't know anyone. She struggled every month to pay the rent and take care of their needs. And while she knew she was called to serve God, she had to give up her dream of traveling with a worship band. "I really thought that my mistakes made me miss out on serving God."

And yet God has blessed her with unexpected open doors. Suzanne joined a church and is now a worship leader and serves on the church board. She knows she is doing God's will every night when she prays with her children before she tucks them into bed.

Suzanne often quotes Psalm 103:12. "As far as the east is from the west, so far has He removed our transgressions from us" (NASB).

"He has proven over and over that He is faithful even when I am not," Suzanne says. "I could never have made that move on my own, but now this place really feels like home for us. When I get discouraged, it's God who reaches down and reassures me of His plan."

Gillian
Saved from the Shipwreck

illian sat on the deck of her boyfriend's boat, drinking champagne, the blue-green tropical water of the Caribbean stretching out in front of her. Her life with John was filled with four-star hotels, spa vacations, and weekends in the country or in New York City for the latest Broadway show. But there was a dark underbelly to this glamorous, romantic life. John could be charming, or he could be vicious—especially if he'd been drinking. "I think I thought somehow my love could help heal him," Gillian says. "I knew he had his own hurts from childhood, and I used that to excuse his behavior. I put up with a lot—like Hansel and Gretel following this trail—to get the little crumbs of love he threw me."

Gillian had grown up in a Christian family and walked the aisle in her Baptist church to give her life to Christ when she was six years old. "I don't know if I really understood what I was doing," she says. In college, her life took a drastic turn. She wanted to belong and to have fun, so the girl who had been a leader in her Christian high school started going to parties—all the time. She started seeing a guy, and they became intimate. "I felt guilty, but not guilty enough to stop."

Greg said he became a Christian (at one level, the faith of

Gillian's upbringing was still important to her), and they made plans to marry. "Six months into the marriage, I wondered what I had done," she says. "I was so unhappy and so focused on myself... I craved affection, and didn't get it at home."

Then Gillian met John, the dashing client at work who lavished her with attention, who told her she was smart and creative and indispensable. Flirting led to late-night conversations on business trips, which led to one kiss, which led to much more. When Gillian told her husband that she needed to spend the night out of town for a business retreat, she had no idea he would follow her. She stayed with John that night, and her husband stayed in her empty hotel room. Understandably hurt, Greg lashed out. He packed up all of Gillian's things and left them on her parents' doorstep. "I was humiliated," she says, "but, at the same time full of pride, unable to simply walk away."

Gillian's story of coming back to God is messy. Years of living life the way she wanted left her feeling sick. "I had bought into so many lies. I didn't know the truth from reality," she explains. She and John broke up and got back together, over and over. She realized that this relationship was broken—he couldn't truly love her, but he still had a hold on her heart.

Through all of this, Gillian's grandmother was praying for her. Once, as they stood at her kitchen sink washing dishes, her grandmother said, "You know, the way you're living is not pleasing to the Lord." Gillian knew this was the voice of love and truth, and while part of her resisted, a small part of her heart was opening up to change.

"I used to think about coming back to church, coming back to God," she says, "but I thought I had to get my life cleaned up first. On the few occasions I went to church, I felt horrible. There were always things that pierced my heart, and I wanted to stay away from that. I used to look around at church and think that none of those guys would be interested in me. I felt like trash." She remembers one occasion when the pastor talked about being a "lamplighter" and using the light of Christ to punch holes in the darkness. All Gillian could think was, *I'm broken. There's not even a flicker left in me.*

But God saw things differently. He reached out to Gillian in the way He knew she would hear Him—through another relationship. "My mom wanted to set me up with a guy from her church. I didn't want to go, but finally I gave in. That was my first real decision to change. I don't know if I could have told you then that I was coming back to God, but that's what it was. I was sick of my life—really, I was sick of being sick of being sick. I knew it wasn't working anymore."

The guy from church ended up being a gorgeous, funny ex-military officer. And while that relationship wasn't long-term, God used it to draw Gillian to Himself. "I think all of this was more about me and the Lord than about this new relationship," she says. "He used my weakness—relationships—to draw me back to Him. He knew I needed something to hold on to."

Almost immediately—in what Gillian sees as a miracle—God closed her heart to John completely. None of his pleading had any effect on her as he showed up in her office in tears, day after day. She began to read her Bible. Very slowly, she started attending church. She pored over Psalms and Isaiah and found hope in their words of healing. She began to understand the lies she had been living by, and Scripture became alive, as though God was giving her new sight, the way He gave sight to the blind. She was being healed.

"I was adrift at sea," Gillian says. "I expected to be shipwrecked, and instead God gently scooped me up. He taught me to trust that His love was enough, and constantly confirmed to me in dozens of small ways that I was doing the right thing."

Gillian moved back home. She got involved in a singles group at a large church and felt fed with spiritual food and with great friendships. "I was convinced I would never be married again, that that would be my punishment because of all the bad decisions I'd made. What God showed me was that it wasn't about punishment, but about making me holy. That was His priority. I believed that He wouldn't do anything that wasn't good for me, and I knew that, with His help, I could be satisfied being single."

Determined to stop flirting and to not manipulate relationships anymore, Gillian got involved in the prayer team and other service opportunities. And that's how she met Kirk—a cute, funny, athletic guy she thought of as a friend. When he asked her out, she thought, *It's not a date; it's just Kirk.* When he told her his intentions—that he wanted to get to know her because he saw characteristics in her that he had always wanted in a wife—Gillian panicked. "I had never done dating the right way," she says. "It was always physical, always about chemistry and electricity. I had no idea how to pursue the right kind of relationship."

Gillian trusted God, even though this relationship was different from any she'd had before. She loved the fact that Kirk's character was spotless, that he was a man who loved God. There were no red flags; there was nothing contrary to God's Word. As they hung out and had fun, their friendship deepened. They went sledding and four-wheeling, had long discussions about Scripture, and Gillian realized that this pure relationship was life-giving. God continued to gently love her, and Kirk did as well—accepting her in spite of her past. A deep and lasting love grew. "The chemistry was definitely there," she says. "I just had to do things in a different order than I'd been used to. I'm so glad I did."

She and Kirk are now married with two little girls. As Gillian reflects, she says, "I want my girls to know that I'm confident in who I am in Christ and that I find my satisfaction in Him. I want to be a mommy who loves Jesus before she loves anything else. I know that's the most important love—the love of God. I'm so thankful He loved me back to Himself."

part six

Faith Crises

In the beginning...

Eve

"The woman said, 'The serpent deceived me, and I ate.'"
—GENESIS 3:13 (NIV)

She's the brunt of a lot of jokes from pastors, stand-up comedians—and lots of husbands. Most people look at her life and think, *How could you have ruined all of history by wanting just a bite of fruit? How could you have turned away from God? How did you live with yourself after what you did?* Eve, it turns out, was the first prodigal, the first woman to turn away from the God who loved her. But she was also the first woman to turn back to Him and discover what unconditional love and forgiveness feel like.

God created Eve, in His wisdom, to be Adam's wife. She really had it all. She knew her Creator and that He loved her. She had a loving husband and one amazing place to live.

Eve's favorite part of the day was probably when God walked through the Garden of Eden with her and Adam, and they would marvel at everything He created for their enjoyment. She loved to watch the multi-colored fish swim and splash in the rivers, and she would sit on the rocks and wonder about the underwater world. God seemed to like it when she noticed things about what He created. The first time she saw the patch of purple flowers that grew overnight, she loved God even more. She was in awe of what He could create.

Adam and Eve had all they needed and were very happy to live in this Paradise. Eve loved God, but she was also human. And because of that, she was vulnerable to the plan of the serpent.

The day it happened began with a leisurely walk around the Garden, maybe looking for more of those purple flowers. She innocently found herself in the middle of the garden where that one forbidden tree was. She paused and remembered God's clear warning: "You may freely eat the fruit of every tree in the garden—except the tree of the knowledge of good and evil. If you eat its fruit, you are sure to die" (Genesis 2:16–17, NLT).

I can't keep my eyes off of its beauty, she confessed to herself. She knew she couldn't eat the fruit. But Eve was fascinated. She wanted to touch it. She faced temptation for the first time in her life, and her thoughts accelerated. *What would happen if, just once, I just . . .*

It was as if the serpent had read her thoughts. Maybe he had. He showed up in the middle of the garden, as if he had been expecting Eve to be there. "Eve, you won't die!" the serpent assured her. "Actually, you will be more like God if you eat it, and you will have new knowledge."

"Really?" she asked, intrigued. *Has God been keeping things from me? Could He really have good reasons to keep this from me, or does He just not love me as much as He says He does?*

Eve didn't need the serpent to continue to convince her. The next thing she knew, she had pulled the fruit off the tree and brought it to share with Adam. He wasn't hard to convince, either. But before they had even swallowed the fruit, they felt different. Neither of them had ever felt shame before. There had been no reason for guilt before that day. All of a sudden, though, they didn't want God to come and visit. They felt naked, a word that had never meant anything to them before.

Eve didn't know how she could face God. She couldn't even face Adam. Her husband, also ashamed, went to a fig tree and sewed the leaves together so they could cover themselves. They waited in tortured anticipation, knowing that God would be coming. Eve realized that by disobeying Him, she had made a choice to turn her back on God. She cried for the first time, feeling the weight of her sin.

The cool evening breezes came, and she heard God walking around in His garden. The Lord said, "Where are you?"

"I heard you walking in the garden, so I hid. I was afraid because I was naked," said Adam. Eve was too afraid to speak. She was the one who had taken the first bite. That made her feel more guilty, somehow.

Her mind was reeling. "The serpent tricked me," is all she could come up with. "That's why I ate it." The excuses sounded clunky and empty as she forced them out.

Their behavior had consequences, as behavior always does. God spoke a curse over both of them and kicked them out of their paradise, the home He had made for them to enjoy. At the time, Eve didn't believe He loved them anymore. Her last glance back at the river was full of regret. Never again would she gaze into its clear pools of water. She would never see those velvety clusters of purple flowers by the water's edge again. She wept as the gates of paradise closed them out, and she knew they were faced with the vast wilderness ahead, where they would live out the curse.

Eve was terrified. Everything was different. Her heart felt different. It felt different being out of God's presence. No longer was she a co-laborer with Adam in the garden with God. They were now sinners, separated from Him.

Her relationship with Adam changed. They fought and struggled to get along. Eve resented him because she thought her husband should have protected her, stopping her evil choice. Adam had let her make the worst decision of her life. And when Adam blamed Eve before God, she instantly found herself wanting to move away from him, and her heart became hardened. Adam wasn't as beautiful to her as before, nor was she to him. *Why didn't God just punish the devil? Did we all deserve a curse, equally?*

As years passed and children came, perhaps Eve understood better why God had kicked them out. He couldn't allow them to stay once they had brought shame and guilt into their lives. He had to fix what was messed up, and that required a Savior. Though she had turned her back on God, He provided a way to restore her. The faces of her children still revealed the image of God, after all.

Adam and Eve managed to make it through a difficult marriage. The serpent still came around, but now Adam and Eve found him much easier to resist. They were filled with regret any time their children were tempted, and they hated to see them fall for his schemes. He still had his beauty and charm, but they knew now he wasn't worth it.

Year after year, even as her guilt affected her every day, Eve was amazed that God continued to show her His grace. He even sent patches of her favorite purple flowers. He didn't remove the curse, but He forgave them. Over and over, He opened His arms to Eve and Adam, who used to walk in His garden, and to their children.

Eve knew she was not worthy of God's grace, but God made it clear that His love was constant—even outside the walls of the Garden. She knew God was big enough to solve the problem of sin, though she didn't know His plan fully. But as she continued to walk with Him, she just knew. Nothing could separate her from her Creator.

Emma
Seeing the Future

*E*mma watched her husband, Brendan, get out of the car and stretch. They'd traveled eighteen hours, not stopping for rest because they couldn't find a motel room. They watched the sunrise standing next to their convertible.

"I don't know how anyone can look at that and say there is no God," Brendan said.

Emma agreed. She took the keys from Brendan and sank into the driver's seat for her turn behind the wheel. Exhausted, she turned on the radio. She remembers reaching for a Pepsi sometime during the drive . . . and then everything went black.

The car flipped three times, each time landing on Brendan. Sirens swirled through the morning air. Paramedics pulled Emma from the car. She argued, "I know my husband's in worse shape. Why won't you take care of him?"

They didn't answer. Just as she was being lifted into the wide mouth of an ambulance, she saw them pull a white sheet over Brendan's body.

"In my mind, I had killed him," she says. "Here he was, a decorated war vet. He'd saved lives, and then was killed on a highway. By me."

But even harder than Brendan's death was Emma's secret

knowledge that she felt a certain amount of relief over Brendan's death. They'd had a tumultuous relationship. Sometimes she wasn't safe from his temper. He'd thrown a plate of spaghetti once, punched his hand through the wall. He'd almost succeeded in shoving her down a flight of stairs, and he hit her once. She didn't know if she wanted to have children with a man like that. When a patrolman asked, "How was your marriage?" after the accident, Emma sunk deeper into her feelings of guilt, which punctured her heart and eroded her faith.

She'd met Jesus when she was nine. She memorized Scripture, attended church three times a week, and sang in the choir. But Emma felt distant from God. In college, she watched other people connect to Jesus emotionally, but she thought they were strange. At the end of her freshman year, after a painful breakup with a soon-to-be-preacher, Emma met Brendan. She married him that year and quit school. God moved further back in her mind and life. Three years later, she was a widow.

Emma's sister came to take care of her after the accident. Her sister had also left the church where the girls had grown up, delving instead into the New Age movement.

Emma listened intently as her sister explained the world. "Obviously the cosmos is speaking to you," she told Emma. She pulled out Emma's astrological charts, showing her that the accident was supposed to happen—she wasn't at fault. The cosmos "insisted" it would happen.

Seeing everything so clearly mapped out helped Emma deal with the guilt and pain. "I question now why it was so easy for me to leave my faith," she says. "But something in me died on that highway."

Emma abandoned Christianity with vigor, and started to party, have sex, and attend New Age seminars and study groups. When she met Kurtis, a Christian businessman who volunteered in his church, she "enlightened" him. "We are gods. We have to work out our own path." Since Kurtis was in his own tumultuous marriage, the words made sense to him. That opened the door to the New Age movement and an affair.

Kurtis and Emma scandalized the church community, particularly Emma's parents, when he got a divorce and they married. A few years later, Emma ventured to an ashram (a New Age commune). The buildings were full of framed pictures of the guru who ran the ashram. Followers had to bow down to him several times a day, dip into a river seven times, pray at odd hours, participate in ceremonial exercises, and meditate. Emma describes the experience as "spiritual vertigo. They were desensitizing me. I lost my sense of what was real and what was right."

Kurtis understood what was happening to Emma. He confronted the guru and removed her from the ashram.

They moved to a new city, where people called Emma an "advanced soul" and sought her out for "past life sessions," where she concocted stories of past lives. In turn, she consulted astrologers and psychics for answers. Because many of the people in their church movement used the name "Jesus" or "God" or the word "atonement," she felt she hadn't truly renounced the faith of her childhood. She was simply more enlightened. She believed the people who confirmed her meandering path by saying things like, "Jesus never intended people to think He was the only way to God." Emma's upbringing felt too confining, while these teachings made sense to her, and they helped her mask the grief she kept buried.

While Emma bought into the messages, Kurtis was still struggling. He knew that Emma's mother, grieving the path the couple was wandering, prayed without ceasing. She pulled him aside from time to time, her eyes penetrating his. "I'm counting on you to bring her back to the church."

After more than a dozen moves and the arrival of two children, Kurtis kept up the appearances. On the other hand, he had friction in his spirit, knowing something wasn't right. He read his Bible in a closet and sought answers. Depressed, he cried, "I need help, Lord."

Finally he sought out Emma. "I have spoken to Jesus," he told her. "He is alive and well. And He is the Lord of our lives."

"What are you thinking?" she shot back. "We've gone beyond all that elementary thinking." But he persisted, and eventually Emma started reading the Bible again.

They moved again and started to attend a church they'd seen on TV. This church seemed alive. "I didn't know you could be that free in the Spirit. For once I could finally feel an emotional connection to God."

After more than a decade of New Age thinking, Emma came back to Jesus. "I knew I had no control over my life: the sin, the healing, anything."

Years later, Emma still loves Jesus. Things have not been perfect. She and Kurtis suffered a painful separation, but reconciled. Emma is constantly grateful that God rescued her from her waywardness. "A lot of what I saw in the New Age movement seemed so real, but I now know it was a counterfeit. It's in the journey where we get our real lessons, not in predicting the future."

Rachel
A Soul Connection

*A*s a baby, Rachel was adopted into a loving and extremely conservative Christian home. Her father was a respected professor at a Christian college, and they lived a mile away in a small town. Rachel's entire life was lived in the shadow and protection of this small community, where everyone knew her because everyone knew her father.

The family went to church every Sunday morning, Sunday night, and Wednesday night. Movies were taboo, as were dancing and drinking of any kind. Women were nearly always expected to wear skirts or dresses. From a young age, Rachel knew that Christianity involved a lot of "dos and don'ts," and that nothing should be questioned. She was simply told what to think and what to believe, and she accepted it, the way she was expected to. "I recognized at some level that there was supposed to be a relationship with Christ," she says, "but I never felt that. I tried to read my Bible and pray because that's what you were supposed to do, but I never had any sense of connection. I was following rules."

Rachel went to college at the school where her father taught, and after she graduated, she started to teach in Christian high schools. But at twenty-one, she began to question things, unsure if Christianity was really for her. She didn't feel prepared for the "real world." People expected her to have everything together because of her father's reputation as a Bible teacher, so she hid her struggles while her faith slowly crumbled inside.

"I felt lonely and disconnected," she says. "I was starting to ask questions I had never asked before. Some of the teachers I worked with weren't particularly welcoming or kind. I thought, *If this is how Christians treat each other, this isn't what I want.*"

Unhappy and tired of faking it, tired of working to read her Bible and pray, of feeling lonely and disconnected, Rachel walked away. She quit teaching and left the church. "My outward rebellion probably wasn't extreme—I got a tattoo and had a few drinks, things that would have given my parents heart attacks—but mentally, I was finished. I wanted no part of that. I didn't think God loved me or heard me. He didn't listen."

While she no longer talked to most of her Christian friends, her closest friend, Deanna, was always there, though their relationship wasn't as deep as it had been. Deanna would tell Rachel from time to time that she was praying for her. But Rachel felt better in her new life. There was no more pretending, no pressure to maintain her family name. Yet after a year, she felt lonely and miserable and decided to start going to church again.

"For me, there was not a particular lightbulb moment. It was more of a process that took years," she says. "When I came back to faith, I wasn't really thrilled to be back, but I figured I would just keep struggling along. I hadn't been happy away from it, and I thought maybe this painful kind of faith would be as good as it ever got."

But when Rachel took a job at a Christian college, she saw something different. "The professors and students there were connected, real, and honest. I realized that whatever they had was what I wanted."

Through counseling and the companionship of a close friend, Rachel was finally able to open up about her struggles. "I remember I told my friend Kara one day that I had a hard time reading my Bible. She said, 'I do, too.' I was shocked! I realize now that lots of people struggle with faith, but few of us talk about it. I finally felt like it was okay to feel stupid, to not get it. I admitted my doubts and questions and asked for advice, and really finally worked through things. There were lightbulb moments for me, one after another."

Working through things meant uncovering memories Rachel never wanted to talk about. As an adopted child, she felt abandoned and rejected by her birth parents. Worse, she had been abused as a young teenager by someone in her small community. She had blocked much of it out, which she views in some ways as God's protection. The one time she had tried to talk about it, her friend hadn't believed her, so she'd never mentioned it again. She courageously told her counselor her story. "Where was God? Why did He allow this to happen? I wanted to know. I had never understood that. He'd abandoned me. She said, 'He was right there with you, interceding for you, mourning with you.' It was the first time I was able to consider that."

Before Rachel started her healing process, she had worked on memorizing 2 Samuel 22:31: "God's way is perfect. All the Lord's promises prove true. He is a shield for all who look to him for protection" (NLT). While it didn't make sense at first, Rachel rests now in the fact that God is the protector of her soul. "There is no pat answer for the difficulty in understanding this verse," she says. "But I see how God protected me from worse outcomes and how He shielded me from more pain. And now I pray that verse, asking God to shield me when Satan wants to play with my mind and put untruthful thoughts there, and to shield me from hurtful feelings when I am with people who have hurt me. I feel totally secure in Him now. It doesn't mean I don't still struggle or doubt at times. I am still in the process of forgiving. But I *know* God is there and that He loves me."

Rachel still appreciates her parents' faith and their desire to raise her in a godly home. "They didn't become Christians until later in life, and when they did, they chose a very conservative church because of their previous life. That was what they needed, and I know they only meant the best for me. But I had to move away from that legalistic approach to faith in order to understand my relationship with God."

Rachel says her relationship with God now is completely different from what she had growing up. "I view Him as a friend and Father, someone I know is compassionate and understanding. There's a soul and heart connection, not just a cold list of things I'm supposed to do. I never really thought it could be like this."

Nadia
Out of Bondage

*I*n Egypt, Islam is the national religion. It is illegal for an Egyptian Muslim to convert to Christianity, but young people from Christian families face pressure to become Muslim. Christian children are warned that groups of extremists dedicate their lives to converting Christians to Islam, to embarrass their families and to weaken Christianity's influence in the country.

Nadia knew all of this; she was the daughter of wealthy Christian parents who were well known in their community. But knowing what might happen is not always enough to prevent it.

Nadia was a beautiful, outgoing college student who read her Bible daily and sang in her church choir. She had many friends, both Christian and Muslim. One day, one of her Muslim friends introduced her to Aarif, a charismatic man who appeared to be Muslim by birth but secular by choice. He told her he was open to all faiths, and engaged her in long conversations about what she believed. He told her that no one had ever explained the Bible or the life of Jesus to him the way she did. He went with her to church on occasion, but he resisted making any commitment. His father and uncle were Islamic clergymen, he told her, and would cause trouble if they thought someone from their own family might convert. "We'll leave it in the hands of God," he assured her. And she believed him.

Nadia's friendship with Aarif developed for a year. Although he told her he was falling in love with her, he respected her faith and did not pressure her into a physical relationship. Before long, Nadia was head over heels in love.

Aarif told her he wanted to convert to Christianity and marry her, but because of the laws and his fear of his family, he would have to move to another country. Nadia offered to elope with him. Christian families in Egypt are very strict, and eloping would be a significant embarrassment. Offering to follow him meant rejecting her parents, but Nadia didn't care.

At Aarif's prompting, she convinced her parents she was going to a convent to pray for several weeks. Instead, the couple took a train to a different city, where Nadia planned to live quietly until they had the money to leave the country.

After only one night together, though, everything changed. Aarif told her they would go out after breakfast to meet some people he knew. As they walked, Nadia started to feel odd—it was hard to move and she couldn't think clearly. Aarif had drugged her food. He took her to Muslim clergymen, who talked to her about Islam and the Qur'an. Instead of Aarif converting to Christianity, he forced her to listen to men bent on converting her!

The drugs did what Aarif wanted them to. Nadia couldn't think clearly enough to make her own decisions, so she obediently met with the clergymen every day for a month. She started to accept that the only way to be with Aarif was to embrace Islam.

Aarif disappeared for weeks at a time, and one day when he returned from one of his unexplained absences, Nadia confronted him.

"I did everything you wanted me to do. I did all this for our love. Now it is time for you to marry me."

Aarif looked at her coldly. "You did not love your religion, so I think you are incapable of loving a man. I cannot marry you, because you have no loyalty." Nadia was shocked. "I left everything behind for your sake!"

"I did you a favor," Aarif said, turning to leave. "I ushered you into the right religion. I was paid to seduce you and bring you here to be converted. You are not the first nor the last Christian I will win for Islam."

The pain was overwhelming. Nadia didn't understand how she could have been so deceived. Aarif had taken everything from her—her family would never get over the shame of her elopement or let her come home. She could not go back to them or to her church. And yet Aarif didn't want her. What could she do?

Nadia saw no way out. Her spirit was broken. If she completed her conversion to Islam, at least she would be allowed to work in one of the Islamic orphanages as a nanny. She would not be thrown into the street to starve, as she imagined her parents doing if they found her.

Her family had realized weeks before that Nadia was not praying at the convent, and they were trying desperately to find her. The Islamic police refused to help; they knew that the religious leaders were trying to convert Nadia, so they stalled and lied and kept her family away. Finally, after Nadia resigned herself to her fate, the authorities let her parents and pastor meet with her once, with police officers and Muslim clerics in the room.

Nadia cried throughout the meeting, but only said, "There is no God but Allah. It is over. Please leave me be and don't be upset with me."

After that, the Muslim leaders kept Nadia from seeing her

family anymore. They changed her name and sent her to work for an orphanage in another part of the country. She was forced to marry a Muslim street vendor, who beat her and treated her like a slave. After nine months, he got tired of her and divorced her. Now she bore the double shame of being a Christian convert and a divorced woman in a conservative, punishing society. She got a job as a maid at a local hospital, where she slept on the floor and ate whatever scraps she found left on patients' trays. It was a shocking fall for the daughter of aristocrats.

Several years passed. Finally a Christian doctor at the hospital took pity on Nadia and invited her to work for him at a clinic. Nadia told him everything. She knew that what she had done was wrong, and that she should never have allowed Aarif or the Muslim clergy to bully her into converting. She had never truly believed in Islam, and she recognized what she had sacrificed by lying to her parents and leaving her church.

"I would do anything to be able to go home," she told him. "I would be a maid in my father's house and sleep on the floor if it meant I could be a Christian."

As Nadia shared her story, the doctor recognized things she said. He had recently met a Christian who talked about how he used to seduce young women into converting to Islam. The Holy Spirit had caught up with the man, and like the apostle Paul on the road to Damascus, he had embraced the love and forgiveness of Jesus Christ. Could this man be Aarif, Nadia's former lover?

The doctor brought the two together, and Nadia recognized Aarif right away. She didn't speak as he wept and begged for forgiveness. He told her his story and promised to approach her parents on her behalf.

Aarif went to Nadia's family, confessing everything and taking full blame for what had happened. Her parents were shocked; they had believed that Nadia had chosen to convert to Islam voluntarily and had no idea how hard their daughter's life had become. Ignoring tradition, they threw their doors open to welcome Nadia back as the daughter they'd lost. Her past didn't matter. All that mattered was that she was once again a follower of Christ and a member of their family.

Nadia moved back to her parents' house and healed slowly. She still has nightmares, and still cries when she thinks about her lost years and the pain she caused. She never remarried, but today lives with her brother and his family, fully committed to a life of prayer and Bible reading. The story of the prodigal son is her favorite Bible passage.

Christine
Uncovering the Truth

*C*hristine and her family always saw themselves as Christians and never meant to stray so far from their faith that they would need to seek forgiveness.

Her first-generation Christian parents were committed to raising their children in a faith-based home. Prioritizing family above everything else, they homeschooled Christine and her younger siblings, shared devotions every day, and tried to protect their children from the painful experiences that had filled their own childhoods. The family attended a large Baptist church, but Christine's parents pulled her out of Sunday school when she was nine, believing that the children's programs distracted her from her family.

Looking back, Christine sees that Satan must have seen the opportunity in the family's isolation. Her parents began to feel discontent and talked about finding a more family-centered community. When someone told them about a "family integrated" church an hour from their home, they decided to check it out.

What they found seemed like paradise. The pastor, Samuel, lived on a sprawling farm where church members gathered. All of the church members homeschooled their children, and they formed a tight-knit community to raise and protect their children. After years of feeling alone, Christine's parents felt they had found the right place to worship and grow.

Christine and her family began to make the hour-long commute every week for Sunday services, and then several times during the week for midweek worship and service projects. Samuel urged them to move. The church family needed to live close to one another to encourage and hold each other accountable, he said, and the church could provide everything they needed. Two years after Christine's family first met Samuel, they sold their home and moved closer to their new family.

Christine dove into their new life, eager to please and to make a place for herself. She became a protégé to Samuel and his wife, volunteering to spend hours at their house, preparing food or cleaning for church gatherings. She felt privileged to be singled out for her pastor's attention, and strove to do everything he asked. He encouraged her adoration, telling her that her parents had a lot to learn about living as Christians, and that Christine should look to Samuel and his wife as her "true" parents.

"Being with Samuel was like spending too much time in direct sun," she explains. "If you sit in the heat too long, you don't have the energy to move. Samuel was like that—if we stayed near him too long, we didn't have the energy to make our own decisions."

Christine didn't immediately see the gradual changes that were happening to the community. A few years after they joined the church, Samuel preached about the way women dressed. Taking Old Testament verses, he declared that women should not wear pants. Christine went home that day and threw away every pair of jeans she owned, horrified that she had ever worn them. She began wearing long skirts and dresses, as did all of the women in the church.

A few months later, Samuel spoke forcefully against women attending college. God's sole purpose for Christine, he told her, was to marry the man of her parents' choice when she was eighteen. When the daughter of a church member enrolled in seminary, Christine joined the rest of the church in shunning her.

Some of her family's old friends came to visit the new church, but expressed concern that the sermons focused more on the roles of men and women than on a relationship with God. Samuel spoke often and at great length about the value of family—which is what drew Christine and her parents in the first place—but Christine does not remember him ever reading from the New Testament or preaching about the life of Jesus during that time.

Christine felt isolated. Samuel kept her busy, kept her limited, and had stopped bringing new members into the church. The body was complete, he said, and they didn't need anyone else bringing in the ideas of the world to "defile" what God had brought together.

Despite all the talk about God during those years, Christine doesn't think she had any kind of personal relationship with Him during that time. "If I spent time thinking about God, I was afraid of Him. We said we lived under grace, but we never practiced it. And Samuel never gave us time to think. He told me he was next to Jesus. I believed him. He took the place of God in my life."

Finally, four years after Christine and her family joined the church, the truth caught up to them. Members became uncomfortable with Samuel's sermons and how the women of the congregation were treated. They examined Scripture themselves and could not find a biblical basis for many of the rules imposed on them.

Christine's father, a deacon in the church, was shocked to

finally see the truth and took the lead in confronting the man who had led them. He and other church members biblically confronted Samuel, who refused to acknowledge what they told him. The charismatic pastor left angrily, and half the congregation followed him.

The rest, shocked and hurt, tried to keep meeting, but in the end acknowledged that a church not built on truth could not stand. At seventeen years old, Christine identified her church as a cult. She was spiritually adrift. "After four years of feeling like these people were our family, everything was ripped away in a week. We were in shock."

The past few years have been an intense time of healing for Christine. While she always thought she was obeying Christ, she realized she needed to build a relationship with Him and repent of the pride that drew her onto the wrong path in the first place.

It was not easy to seek forgiveness from a God she was taught to fear, but gradually, she met the true God who loves her. A few months after her family left the church, she went for a walk alone and stopped by a pond. "I prayed for open eyes and a real relationship with Christ. And in that moment, God gave me a bird's-eye view of where I had been, and where He was waiting for me all this time," she says with wonder. "I stood there with every scar showing, every piece of me that had been covered by long skirts and long hair and long hours of work. And I knew that He saw me and loved me. I knew I didn't have to dress a certain way to impress God or get into heaven."

Christine has embraced God's love. Today she is involved with the church she attended before she and her family joined Samuel's group, and is planning to attend college. She radiates joy and the assurance that she is loved, and she holds on to Joel 2:25, where God promises to "repay you for the years the locusts have eaten" (NIV). For Christine, the future is full of grace.

Summer
Feeling the Hand of the Lord

Summer never consciously made a decision to walk away from God. Looking back, she sees it more as a series of little slips and slides away from God's people, and then away from God, and into a place where there was no hope.

As a child, Summer was surrounded by people who taught her the Bible. She accepted Christ as her Savior when she was seven because she was afraid of going to hell if her parents would not be there. God was "a big brother who lived in another city," she explains. "He was always reachable, but I didn't want to disturb Him."

The Bible was an academic subject to Summer, who went to a Christian school for most of her growing-up years. The kids in her church's youth group didn't help her find the real Jesus. Week after week, she felt out of place, like "the geek trying to get into the jocks' group," and eventually she looked for ways to stop going.

There were two places Summer felt comfortable: at her part-time job at a restaurant, and with the many pets at her ranch home. Over time, Summer started to let those two things take priority in her life. Her daily devotions and Bible reading kept her from working and playing with her animals, so she quit doing them. And she started requesting to work instead of going to youth group meetings, and then started working on Sunday mornings so she could skip church, too.

Working on Sundays showed Summer a different side of the church people who had always surrounded her. "Sunday mornings are the worst day to work. Just after the local churches get out, [the restaurant] gets a rush of dressed-up, crabby people." Disillusioned by the behavior of people who claimed to share her faith, and feeling guilty about her own distance from the church, Summer lashed out. "I started to view Christians as hypocrites... and I didn't think much of their God. I thought it was silly of people to believe that He cared about their problems. Christians were just [mean] adults with an imaginary friend."

Summer's increasing frustration with her faith started to affect her relationship with her parents. When her mother tried to talk to her about the changes in her behavior, Summer attacked her with hot, angry words. She developed a sarcastic response to anything related to Christianity or faith.

"Yeah, I might be going to hell," she would tell her mother bitterly, "but at least then I'll be warm." She had no interest in "soaring like an eagle" the way the Bible described the lives of Christians, because as the saying goes, "At least weasels don't get sucked into jet engines."

Summer provoked her parents to anger time after time, and when they tried to apologize and rebuild the relationship, she swore and physically pushed them away. Many nights she fled to her room, where she could be alone and cry. She surrounded herself with animals and tried to avoid people—especially Christians. She started to hang out with the "bad crowd" at school, but didn't let them get too close to her. (In hindsight, this distance probably protected her from much worse experiences;

today, most of Summer's high school friends have been arrested for theft or drug dealing.)

Her rebellion from God and her increasing issues with anger came to a painful end on a dark night when Summer collapsed in her room, devastated after a difficult talk with the veterinarian. Her beloved dog, her best friend and companion, was dying. Summer felt like Holly was closer to her than family, and as she contemplated moving forward with her alienated parents and distant friends, she was overwhelmed by loneliness.

"At that point, I decided I'd had enough of life."

Summer had never considered suicide before, never given her family any warning that her emotions could be that out of control. But she had abandoned God and hurt her parents terribly, and at that moment Summer wanted nothing more than to end the pain.

She took a knife from the kitchen and carried it to her room. But when she tried to lift it to her wrists, the knife would not move. It was as if there were another hand on Summer's, holding the weapon away from her. Summer was filled with the knowledge that the same God she'd accused of being an imaginary friend, the same God she'd said didn't care about people and didn't get involved in their lives—that same God had just sat in her room and kept her from hurting herself. He was real, and He did care, and she had just experienced Him in a bright, tangible way.

Summer threw the knife away from her and began to cry. And over her tears, she heard a voice. "I have plans for you." Summer recognized the words from a verse she'd memorized in Sunday school years before: Jeremiah 29:11: " 'For I know the plans I have for you,' says the Lord, 'plans to prosper you and not to harm you, plans to give you hope and a future' " (NIV).

Summer's life changed that night. She never again lashed out at her parents or other Christians about their faith. She never again doubted the truth of Scripture or the reality of God. She had met Him, and He had remained faithful to her.

Today, Summer trains horses on her family's farm. She is currently working with a challenging foal that remains stubborn even as Summer tries to gently lead him and prepare him for his future. She understands the parallel to her own experiences: just as she cannot train a horse without adding some pressure, God needed to put some challenges in Summer's path in order to form her into the person He wanted her to be. She thanks God every day that He so patiently waited and so lovingly met her when she most needed Him.

Debbie
Waiting for God to See Things Her Way

*D*ebbie was home alone, trying to fall asleep in the dark, quiet house, wondering if her sister would live. Kate was in the hospital with tubes running out of her arms, unable to sit up on her own. Debbie's parents sat by Kate's side—their new place of residence—waiting for answers.

Kate had been normal, full of life, until she'd caught a mysterious illness. She was losing her ability to function. Would Kate die? Debbie didn't know. But she knew she was tired of being alone.

As much as Debbie loved her sister, she wanted her junior high life back and her family back more than anything else. Her parents were consumed with trying to find the right doctors and the right treatment. Their happy family—with their vacations and soccer games and dinner together almost every night—was falling apart. Debbie knew about the love and sovereignty of God, but couldn't reconcile that with what was happening. How could God allow this? Where could she go to stop being afraid, to find some sense of security again? Her comfort had been torn away, and she no longer felt God could be trusted.

So Debbie decided to avoid God until He started to see

things her way. She stopped going to youth group and got more involved with her boyfriend, David. When her parents made her go to church anyway, she sat stone cold, determined not to hear anything or participate in any way. Finally, when she left for college—with her sister still dangerously ill and now completely disabled—she felt free to live life the way she wanted. She started binge drinking, partying, and sleeping with David. The parties in her dorm lasted until four o'clock in the morning and were often broken up by police or paramedics. While Debbie still carried some sense of conviction, she loved her freedom and wanted nothing to do with God.

"In my heart I was very dissatisfied. I was living in that pigsty, like the prodigal son who squandered his inheritance and lost everything of value. No one else could see it, but I could."

From the outside, Debbie's life looked perfect—great grades, parties, a social life, a loving boyfriend, good friends. Inside, she knew differently. She started to think about God again from time to time, but David—who had left the church as Debbie had—didn't want to go down that path. "I had no answers," she says. "And this was something David couldn't fix. I think I wanted him to be my god, essentially, because I felt God had failed me. But I began to realize this relationship wasn't what I thought it was."

Even with that dissatisfaction, turning back to God was not appealing. "I didn't want to come back to God. I didn't even *want* to want to come back," Debbie says. "That was when God in His great love stepped in and changed me."

On a Saturday afternoon, Debbie drove out into the California countryside for the wedding shower of an old friend. The girls had grown in their faith together and loved each other, but they hadn't met for years. "I don't really know what happened," she says, "but on the drive home, my life changed, and I knew it.

We hadn't talked about anything convicting, and I hadn't even told them what was going on in my life. If anything, maybe I sensed their inner joy. I knew that was fully available to me, but I had turned away from it. I saw what running my own life looked like; I knew I wasn't able to do it on my own. I knew I couldn't continue turning my back on God, that I couldn't continue with all that bitterness."

Debbie attributes that life-changing moment to the power of the Holy Spirit. "I have no explanation for it, other than that the Holy Spirit started tearing down the walls I had built up so fervently," she says. "He brought me to my knees on that drive home. Though I never doubted that God was there and waiting for me, and I knew that all I needed to do was repent, I didn't have the strength to do it on my own."

Debbie knew as well that God was asking her to give some things up—most of all, her boyfriend and the drinking and partying she loved. Over the next year, her conviction grew, and her small steps toward God became major life changes.

"I remember sitting with my boyfriend, breaking up with him, and it was as if I were watching it from the outside. There was no way I had the strength to do that on my own. I had let my heart become so entangled with this boy that ripping it away seemed impossible. But nothing is impossible with God." Debbie cried for weeks, but she was full of relief and joy that she was being obedient to God.

She went back to church, sitting in the back and leaving right after the service was over. She delved into Scripture on her own and felt God opening her eyes. "I realized I could walk away from all of that, that I was a new creation." God surrounded Debbie with comfort, too—and with Christian friends who were actually fun. "I didn't expect that," she says. "I thought they would be boring. These were people I actually wanted to hang out with!"

Debbie finished college and is pursuing her graduate degree. She plans to work with special-needs children, helping place them in the best educational programs to meet their needs. When she's not in school, she helps care for Kate, whom doctors have been unable to help. "It's still challenging and frustrating, and I'm even angry at God sometimes," she says. "I may have to take care of her for the rest of my life. But in some way I can't really explain, I know that all of this—the trials, the heartache, the pain—is because God loves me, that in some way, this is His love in our lives. I know that He does use all things for good, and I'm able to rest in His love."

In so many ways, Debbie feels surrounded by God's love. "God's conviction in my life *was* His love for me. I had worked myself into this mud pit. He came in to pull me out, even though I fought Him every step of the way."

One of Debbie's theme passages now is Habakkuk 3:18–19: "Yet I will rejoice in the LORD; I will take joy in the God of my salvation. GOD, the Lord, is my strength; he makes my feet like the deer's; he makes me tread on my high places" (ESV). She explains, "Now, because of God's graciousness, even if my life crumbles and falls the way Habakkuk's did, I can still say that."

Emily
Journey of a Thousand Steps

*A*s a child, Emily longed for God, but Christianity was a mystery to her, and she couldn't find anyone to explain it. Her grandmother was a committed Christian, but her parents had turned away from their faith and no longer took the family to church.

In first grade, a boy told her, "If you don't believe in God, you're going to hell." She told him, "Yeah, but I believe in God," and she did. She just didn't have any idea how to get close to Him.

In middle school, one of Emily's friends asked her about her faith. "I'm a Baptist because my grandmother is a Baptist," Emily said.

Her friend replied, "You need to be a Christian."

"But how?" Emily wondered.

"Get right with God!" her friend said with confidence.

"I had no idea how to get right with God, or what that even meant," Emily says. "I knew I wanted to do it, though."

Emily recounted that story to her brother. Even though he wasn't a Christian, he gave her the first helpful piece of spiritual advice she'd received: "Read Matthew, Mark, Luke, and John," he said. So she delved into the first four books of the New Testament. She read one chapter of her King James Version every week, and didn't understand any of it.

Finally one Mother's Day, when Emily was in high school, her grandmother requested that the whole family join her for church. "The youth pastor was a former football player," Emily says. "I thought that was so cool. My parents let me go to youth group, and by the end of the summer, I understood faith in God—I knew that I had sinned, that God had paid the price of my sin with Jesus' death, and that all I had to do was accept His grace. So I did. I was thrilled."

Quiet and shy, Emily told some of her friends about Christ. "I wasn't obnoxious about it," she says, "but it was something I had to talk about. I did lose some friends and I wasn't invited to some parties, but I was so excited about my new faith. There were days I was even late for the bus because I was reading my Bible. It all made sense now, and I immersed myself in it."

After high school, Emily went to a Christian college and studied music—her lifelong passion. "It was a dynamic opportunity to grow," she says. "Everyone there was so loving and compassionate. I learned so much about God and absolutely loved it."

She went on to seminary after college, and ironically, that is where her lifelong pursuit of God began to falter. "I was at a very conservative school and was miserable, but I felt God wanted me there and I didn't feel like I could leave."

Emily felt as if the school didn't fully support her vision for ministry because she was a woman and they believed women's ministry roles should be limited. In hundreds of small ways, she started to feel judged, as if she were of less value than the guys she went to classes with. She met and became engaged to Daniel, a seminary student who planned to be a pastor or college minister.

"I think I allowed myself to be bitter," she says. "I didn't really feel the grace of God there. I felt confined and restricted. I had chosen to live by their standards while I was in seminary, but I started to rebel. And because I associated their attitudes with the Spirit of God, I felt like I was rebelling against God."

Emily's rebellion wasn't obvious for a long time. But her unhealthy relationship with Daniel eventually pushed her over the edge. Her fiancé could be kind and sweet, but she thought he could also be manipulative and authoritative. He would tell her, "If you disagree with me, you're disagreeing with God." Daniel blamed Emily if they compromised their standards at all physically, telling her she was being too "seductive" and bringing him down. Emily believed that Daniel wanted her to think he was closer to God than she was, and Emily needed to learn to submit to him as her future husband.

After a messy few years, Emily and Daniel broke up. Emily finished seminary, but her heart had become closed to God. "Part of me was full of reckless anger. I felt as if they—my professors, Daniel—spoke for God, and I didn't measure up." Emily stepped back from her faith in subtle ways, no longer reading her Bible and praying, and only going to church to meet friends. She started to drink too much from time to time.

Deeply hurt, she plunged into clinical depression. "I felt cursed. There was a black hole that followed me all the time. I didn't want to go anywhere or talk to anyone. I was searching for one moment of emotional peace." As if that weren't enough, Emily felt guilty for being depressed. "The guilt was huge for me. I didn't think I should need help, and antidepressants weren't really looked at kindly in the Christian world I had been in. Did I even deserve help? I didn't know."

For two years, Emily's closest friends prayed for her. And slowly, God healed her depression and opened her heart. "I know it sounds crazy, but God spoke to me through colors, and I started to meditate on the way God describes Himself in [Psalm 12] as keeping us safe." One day, talking to a friend who had also fallen away, Emily suddenly felt as if she'd grasped the love God had for her. "In that moment, I saw so clearly that God loved my friend *so* much, and because I could see His love for her, I knew He loved me that way, too. Immediately I felt and understood God's love. Eventually, I realized that maybe God hadn't been the problem, and maybe the church—however well-meaning—doesn't always speak for Him, she says.

"Eventually I realized that *I* was the one who had fallen away from God, not the other way around. Though I lost faith in God, God never lost faith in me. It only took something small—my single crawl, my opening my heart up to Him—and He was right there to welcome me home."

Conclusion

You Are Loved

"There was once a man who had two sons. The younger said to his father, 'Father, I want right now what's coming to me.'

"So the father divided the property between them. It wasn't long before the younger son packed his bags and left for a distant country. There, undisciplined and dissipated, he wasted everything he had. After he had gone through all his money, there was a bad famine all through that country and he began to hurt. He signed on with a citizen there who assigned him to his fields to slop the pigs. He was so hungry he would have eaten the corncobs in the pig slop, but no one would give him any.

"That brought him to his senses. He said, 'All those farmhands working for my father sit down to three meals a day, and here I am starving to death. I'm going back to my father. I'll say to him, Father, I've sinned against God, I've sinned before you; I don't deserve to be called your son. Take me on as a hired hand.' He got right up and went home to his father.

"When he was still a long way off, his father saw him. His heart pounding, he ran out, embraced him, and kissed him. The son started his speech: 'Father, I've sinned against God, I've sinned before you; I don't deserve to be called your son ever again.'

"But the father wasn't listening. He was calling to the servants, 'Quick. Bring a clean set of clothes and dress him. Put the family ring on his finger and sandals on his feet. Then get a grain-fed heifer and roast it. We're going to feast! We're going to have a wonderful time! My son is here—given up for dead and now alive! Given up for lost and now found!' And they began to have a wonderful time."

LUKE 15: 11–24, THE MESSAGE

*B*ad choices. We all make them—even those of us who know Jesus are not immune to the temptations of sin. Our emotions take over, and we lose sight of what really matters—a Father who loves us and a future with Him in heaven.

Perhaps you have felt the same longing as the son in Luke 15, to step out of the family of God and see what life is like for everyone else. If so, beware. Once a person sets off to sin, there's no way to control what happens next. The freefall life of a prodigal moves you away from God, at speeds that are rapidly beyond your control. And what seemed innocent or exciting before will seem like a disaster once you hit the bottom of the pit and can see clearly how far you've fallen.

If you've already made the leap and turned your back on family or faith, or if you know someone who is in the middle of a prodigal experience right now, there is hope. God does not leave us wallowing in our guilt and bad choices. He forgives us, even when we don't deserve it, because none of us is worthy of forgiveness, no matter how good our lives seem on the outside. And yet God forgives us every time we ask, thoroughly and extravagantly. He waits for us to make the choice to turn toward

Him, broken and battered and full of guilt, and then He meets us with arms outstretched, eager to forgive the big sins and the little ones. God does not force Himself on us. But He meets us wherever we are, whenever we are ready to call on Him.

If you saw yourself in any of the stories you read here, remember that each one of them ended with hope, forgiveness, and relationships renewed. God met these women in the pits where they had fallen, and He loved them through the often slow process of rebuilding their lives. He can do the same for you. He is ready to welcome you home, to stand in the gap between you and the pain, and to be your constant companion in the dark hours. He loves you.

Notes

Part Three, In the beginning:

1. Sue and Larry Richards, *Every Woman in the Bible* (Nashville, TN: Nelson, 1999), 278, 283.

2. Abraham Kuyper, *Women of the Old Testament*, as quoted in *All the Women of the Bible* by Herbert Lockyer (Grand Rapids, MI: Zondervan, 1967).

Author Bios

Australian-born **Rebecca St. James** has won a Grammy Award and multiple Dove Awards, with record sales in the multimillions. A gifted songwriter, Rebecca's signature blend of modern pop/rock sensibilities and lyrics of unwavering devotion has blazed the way to seventeen Top 10 singles—nine of which to date have reached the #1 spot on the charts. She is consistently named "Favorite Female Artist" in Contemporary Christian Music by readers of *CCM Magazine*, and has received RIAA certified gold album awards for her groundbreaking album *God* and her Grammy Award–winning project, *Pray*.

Rebecca is the author or editor of ten books, including *Sister-Freaks*, her first compilation of real-life stories; the best-selling *Wait for Me*; and her most recent devotional, *Pure*. As an actress, she toured as Mary Magdalene in the rock opera musical, *!Hero*, and voiced the character of Hope the Angel in VeggieTales's best-selling DVD production, *The Easter Carol*. As a passionate supporter of and in-demand international spokesperson for the child relief work of Compassion International, Rebecca has been influential in the sponsorship of more than 30,000 of the world's neediest children.

Find out more about Rebecca St. James online at www.rsjames.com or www.myspace.com/rebeccastjames.

Mary E. DeMuth is an author and speaker who loves to help people turn their trials into triumphs. Some of her books include *Authentic Parenting in a Postmodern Culture, Daisy Chain: A Novel,* and the memoir *Thin Places.* A mother of three, Mary lives with her husband, Patrick, and their three children in Texas. You can meet her at www.marydemuth.com.

Elizabeth Jusino indulges in her love for good books and better writing as a literary agent with Alive Communications, where she represents and serves a number of best-selling and up-and-coming authors. She moonlights as a freelance writer, teaches regularly at writing conferences across the country, and not-so-regularly leads business writing and marketing seminars. She and her husband, Eric, live in the Denver area.

Tracey D. Lawrence is a freelance writer and founder of *Scribe Ink, Inc.* She holds a B.S. in Christian Education, an M.A. in Church History and Theology, and is currently working on her D.Phil. Some of her releases include *A Savvy Christian's Guide to Life, CounterCultural Christians* featuring Chuck Colson, and *SisterFreaks.* Tracey lives with her husband, Noel, and son, Jack Brennan, in Denver, Colorado. Visit www.scribeink .com for more information about her work.

Jennifer Schuchmann is the co-author *of Nine Ways God Always Speaks, Six Prayers God Always Answers,* and *Your Unforgettable Life.* She has contributed to *The Church Leader's Answer Book* and the *Couples' Devotional Bible.* She holds an MBA from Emory University, and a bachelor's degree in psychology from the University of Memphis. Jennifer and her husband, David, have one son and live in Atlanta. www.jenniferschuchmann.com

Lori Smith is a freelance writer and the author of *A Walk with Jane Austen: A Journey into Adventure, Love & Faith.* An

Austen addict and travel lover, Lori took a monthlong trip to follow Austen's life through England and write about both Jane's life and her own. Her first book, *The Single Truth*, provided a thoughtful Christian perspective on living a single life. Lori lives in northern Virginia with her sweet, stubborn black lab, Bess. Find more about Lori at www.followingausten.com.

If you liked *Loved*,

check out
Sister Freaks

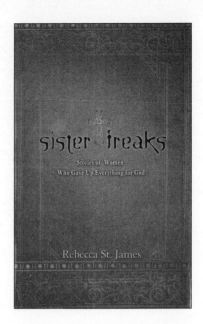

Bestselling author and award-winning singer Rebecca St. James brings together a group of inspirational true stories about young women who gave their all for Jesus. Around the world, every day, these women are boldly putting themselves forth as believers—regardless of the cost. Sometimes they suffer for it, but they never waver in their belief that God has called them to serve Him.

Sister Freaks profiles both contemporary women and historical figures—from Joan of Arc, to a Midwest high school student, to an Olympic athlete. Their stories are sometimes extreme but always inspiring. Divided into thirteen weeks, the book features five profiles each week, thought-provoking questions, and space for journaling.

Rebecca St. James has inspired thousands with her music. Now, she empowers them with these very real, godly role models in whose footsteps they can follow.

Available in bookstores now!

And you'll love

Pure

Rebecca St. James's messages of abstinence and modesty reflect her passionate love for Jesus and her commitment to living for Him. Rebecca does more than talk the talk—she walks the walk. And in this daily devotional, she offers young women the encouragement they need to join her in living a life of all-out purity. It's not just about sex. It's about mind, body, and spirit.

This ninety-day devotional proves that purity is anything but old-fashioned and boring. It's edgy and relevant. Rebecca lives it—and readers can live it too. It starts with Day 1 . . . and ends with everyday radical living.

Available in bookstores now!